Reflec

Reflections on *Empire*

ANTONIO NEGRI

With contributions from
Michael Hardt and Danilo Zolo

Translated by Ed Emery

polity

First published in Italian as *Guide* © Raffaello Cortina
Editore, 2003

This English edition © Polity Press, 2008

Polity Press
65 Bridge Street
Cambridge CB2 1UR, UK.

Polity Press
350 Main Street
Malden, MA 02148, USA

ISBN-13: 978-07456-3704-4
ISBN-13: 978-07456-3705-1 (pb)

A catalogue record for this book is available from the British Library.

Typeset in 11 on 13 pt Plantin
by SNP Best-set Typesetter Ltd, Hong Kong
Printed and bound in Great Britain by MPG Books Ltd, Bodmin, Cornwall

For further information on Polity, visit our website: www.polity.co.uk

Contents

A Note on the Text

This set of working notebooks is organized as follows:

(a)   Five lessons, plus an introduction, delivered at the Institute of Sociology, University of Cosenza-Arcavacata, in the late spring of 2002;

(b)   Each of these lessons has an appendix containing additional working materials, supplementing the content and suggesting further reading.

I see this *Guide* as a set of 'Working Notebooks', in the same way that some of my earlier books were also produced as the outcome of a series of meetings (for instance *Marx beyond Marx*, *Thirty-Three Lessons on Lenin*, and *Insurgencies: Constituent Power and the Modern State*, which were all written with the involvement of others – students, comrades, researchers and so on). It contains analysis and reflection that has been developed through debate and within the movement. This means that each of these notebooks has its own particular historical setting. These latest lessons can also be seen as *setting the stage* . . . as the scenery framing the show. However, as in the case of avant-garde theatre ever since the days of the Russian Ballet, the stage setting has become part of the show . . .

The individual lessons contained in this book were first published by Rubbettino and distributed within the University of Cosenza. I take this opportunity to thank Professor Giordano Sivini, director of the Institute of Sociology at the University of Cosenza, for giving permission for the re-publication by Editore Raffaello Cortina. I also thank Professor Danilo Zolo and Michael Hardt for permission to republish texts that we worked on collaboratively. In addition, I would like to thank the journals and cultural institutions which published previous versions of some of the supplementary texts contained in this volume.

Antonio Negri

1

PREFACE

A Few Concepts Explained

In these lessons I hope to highlight and develop a number of points in the research methodology that led to the writing of *Empire* (Harvard University Press, Cambridge MA and London, 2000). In an article which appeared in a German newspaper in early 2002, the reviewer described *Empire* as 'the idea of globalization raised to the concept'. The Germans are great ones for metaphysics! In fact, yes, the methodology that we (Michael Hardt and I) have set in motion does indeed intend to reach the concept, but a concept that is in no sense idealistic, *pre*conceptual or metaphysical: it is called 'the common name' [*nome comune*]. Our method is very materialist: we name things that are happening, and then, working empirically, we give them more or less general meanings. In so doing we attempt to qualify the extension of the generality at which the definition arrives.

In Lesson 1 I shall attempt to locate the category of 'Empire' in historical terms. I shall then examine *research practices* in relation to causal processes and historical periodization.

Lesson 2 will define the social ontology that underpins the definition of Empire. This ontology is determined by the social transformations that have taken place both in the world of work (the tendential transition to a hegemony of immaterial labour, in other words the transition *from Fordism to post-Fordism*), and in politics (the transition to a new social composition, to a new interconnectedness of the production, reproduction and circulation of goods and signs, on a stage which we refer to as the biopolitical).

Lesson 3 will deal with topics that are more specifically political, offering a definition of the concepts of *the multitude* and *constituent power*, which are born within, and exist in complementary fashion within, the discourse about Empire.

Lesson 4 will examine a more general question: the *production of subjectivity* as such. We shall attempt to understand how the multitude and constituent power can subjectively be part of the ontological constitution of a new world, built from the bottom upwards. What does constituent method mean in everyday reality and within life, within production and as a political expression of the multitude?

The fifth and final lesson presents an analysis of the *logic of research* as a logic that directly implies action. In other words it inserts the moment of praxis into the episteme, and thus it inserts ethics and politics into the processes of knowing.

We finished writing *Empire* in 1997. When you read it in the light of the political realities of the world as it exists now, it is obvious that the book does not deal with various issues which today have become fundamental: on the one hand, the very strong American push towards unilateralism of imperial action; on the other, the perfecting of mechanisms of control that tend towards, and occasionally are inherent within, war. We say that today it is *war* that constitutes sovereignty and sovereign politics, just as yesterday they were constituted by *discipline* and *control*, to adopt a Foucauldian typology of power. Today war is totally inherent in the sovereign body. It is not simply an add-on, like the third stage of a missile (after discipline and control): it is the entirety of it, the outer shell of the Russian doll which is the container for the other techniques of command. These are new elements which will have to be examined more closely if we want to bring our method to life and understand how, and against what, subjectivity continuously needs to assert itself.

Anyway, before addressing these issues, allow me to outline two or three basic theses that underpin the argument developed in *Empire*.

The first is that there is *no globalization without regulation*. There is no economic order or trade regime that does not require some form of regulation. We do not accept the liberal myth of the 'invisible hand', in other words a supposedly providential force that regulates a market that has no subject. There are always hands, active hands, and rules which may be more or less visible but which are always efficacious and manipulatory, operating in the market and everywhere in society. One cannot view the market, let alone globalization, as being somehow disembodied. People offer examples to demonstrate the contrary: the classic one is the operation of the *lex mercatoria*; this is supposed to show the existence of an independent sphere of relations between multinational and international companies, whose regulation takes place almost entirely outside of any validation by national legislations. But this example actually shows quite the opposite – the extent to which, even in fields where private initiative is nearly totally free, regulations are still an absolute necessity: they are, of course, private regulations (their source is to be found in the law firms), but they are nonetheless regulations which aim to be general, and in some respects to replace (and stand in for) state regulation. This is particularly evident in moments of crisis, when the old sovereign power of the state is urgently and desperately called upon to intervene by those selfsame 'free powers' of the market. A typical example is what happened after 11 September 2001, when, especially in fields such as transportation and insurance, the intervention of the US state was absolutely necessary in order to prevent disaster. Another example, particularly relevant today, is the Enron case. It has become paradigmatic of the necessity for regulation – no longer simply a regulation that can be carried out via independent operators (for instance the auditing function entrusted to the Arthur Andersen agency), but a control which is over-determined, a rule that applies to all, to combat the corruption that is endemic in all big organizations (witness the complicity of the Andersen agency, for example). Our first point, therefore, is that there is no globalization without regulation.

Our second thesis is that *the sovereignty of the nation-state is in crisis*. In other words, sovereignty is shifting away from the nation-state and is going somewhere else. The problem is to define precisely where it is going, and this is a problem which remains unsolved. This is why we say that imperial sovereignty is to be found in a 'non-place'. What we are sure of, however, is that there is an effective transfer of the sovereignty of the nation-state into forms that are entirely different from the traditional ones. This is plainly revealed in the crisis of international law of the Westphalian type, i.e. of the system of international law that was founded on a relationship between nation-states, which established between them a series of accords, treaties and contracts and envisaged a set of sanctions in the event of these accords being in some way broken or offended against.

A subordinate problem to that of the crisis of national sovereignty and its eventual imperial transfer is the nature of *borders* and the various striations that our world presents to us. The global world is a striated world. It is a world traversed by continuous divisions, both horizontal and vertical – in other words related to hierarchies of power. At the same time, these striations are becoming increasingly mobile and dynamic. (A while ago I was talking with a fifty-year-old professor of sociology from Ljubljana – today in Slovenia, but yesterday in Yugoslavia. He told me: 'In my life I have seen frontiers increasing at the same rate as the world was becoming unified.') In short, the nation-state is in crisis. And while we wouldn't want to say that the nation-state is finished, at least we have to say that it has lost some of its fundamental prerogatives. At one time national sovereignty was defined as a monopoly in the exercise of power, exercised over a territory that was united by a single culture. Today we can no longer say this, because, precisely, the most basic elements of sovereignty (the exercise of military power, the coining of currency, cultural exclusivity and so on) no longer apply at a national level. This loss has a specific genealogy, which is revealed in the inability of the nation-state to maintain control over the totality of its territory and over the antagonistic forces which move within that territory. At that point, confronted by these forces, the nation-state is forced to resort to other sources of sovereignty. So the issue is not to say that the nation-state is finished, but to show how it becomes transformed once it undergoes a transfer of some of its fundamental powers (such as the power to make war or to mint currency). In matters of culture, language and media too, the nation-state no longer enjoys centrality, because it is continuously traversed by antagonistic currents and by a multiverse of linguistic and cultural inputs that deprive it of the possibility of asserting itself as hegemonic and as exercising command over the cultural process.

We have therefore a reproposition of lines of division on the surface of the globe, in forms that do not have the substantiality of those of the old national and constitutional law: territory, the exercise of sovereignty and language all become elements (and, even more so, concepts) that are shifting and transient. Furthermore we find ourselves facing a misconceived, inadequate, sometimes frankly inconsistent, and almost always new and highly effective use of the concept of *hierarchy*. For example, we always used to describe the world in terms of the classic distinction between First World, Second World and Third World. But this division, too, is becoming less and less a division running along traditional lines, with defined borders. The North–South dichotomy is no longer such a clear-cut thing. Sometimes in the First World we find situations that are effectively Third-World (for instance the *banlieues* of the European metropolises, or the rundown centres of some big American cities), and, at the same time, in areas that used to be described as Third-World you find skyscrapers going up, and you see the emergence of a new capacity of governing, and new powers that are increasingly tied to the First World. Today, extreme poverty sits side by side with wealth, in geographies that are completely new. The key mechanisms of control which at one time operated via geographic divisions are becoming increasingly immaterial. *Frontiers are produced functionally and continuously* – as are the nexuses of hierarchy.

Faced with these phenomena of globalization, the political-constitutional literature is obviously divided on several fronts. The major problem that people have addressed could be categorized under the heading 'globalization and democracy' – in other words, what is the relationship between the transformations arising out of globalization and the forms of democracy that follow from them? In short, how do we identify the relationships and/or dynamics of power that are brought about in the course of globalization, and how do we relate them to the development of democracy?

In addressing this issue I follow a schema that has been elaborated by Michael Hardt. In order to classify the very different positions that have emerged around this question, we have chosen a *fourfold* classification: first there is the division between those who argue that globalization strengthens and develops democracy and those who argue that it blocks or inhibits democracy. These two counterpositions are then divided again, since both positions – the optimistic and the pessimistic – can be seen from either the 'right' or the 'left'. This gives four separate positions:

(1)   The classic social democratic position

Paul Hirst and Grahame Thompson (*Globalization in Question: The International Economy and the Possibilities of Governance*, Polity Press, Cambridge, 1999) give the clearest formulation of this position: globalization is a myth if it excludes the nation-state; globalization gets its power only from the development of the nation-state; furthermore it is only within the framework of the nation-state that a democratic politics can be conducted. This position also contains another one, again social democratic in origin, which maintains that the decline of national sovereignty weakens or removes the protections previously constructed within the nation-state with a view to favouring society against the demands of capital. This position is widely shared by trade union organizations, and also by broad layers of the more radical left within the Western democracies. (David Korten, *When Corporations Rule the World*, Kumarian Press, West Hartford, CT, 1996; Richard Barnet and John Cavanagh, *Global Dreams: Imperial Corporations and the New World Order*, Simon & Schuster, New York, 1994; William Greider, *One World, Ready Or Not. The Manic Logic of Global Capitalism*, Simon & Schuster, New York 1997; R. J. Barry Jones, *The World Turned Upside Down? Globalization and the Future of the State*, Manchester University Press, Manchester, 2000).

(To the social democratic position we should add the thesis – basically argued for in studies deriving from Third Worldism – that globalization means the expansion of US imperialism and, in cultural terms, of Eurocentrism. (Fernando Coronil, 'Towards a critique of globalcentrism', in *Public Culture*, vol. 12, no. 2, spring 2000, pp. 351–74; Arif Dirlik, *Postmodernity's Histories*, Rowman & Littlefield, Lanham, MD, 2000; Fredric Jameson, 'Globalization and Political Strategy', in *New Left Review*, no. 4, July–August

2000, pp. 49–68; Gayatri Spivak, *A Critique of Postcolonial Reason*, Harvard University Press, Cambridge, MA, 1999; Dipesh Chakrabarty, *Provincializing Europe*, Princeton University Press, Princeton, 2000).

So that gives us what we might call the 'globalization versus democracy' position as viewed from the left.

(2) The position of liberal cosmopolitanism

Many writers, and here we refer essentially to Richard Falk, David Held and Ulrich Beck (R. Falk, *Predatory Globalization*, Blackwell, Oxford, 1999; D. Held, *Democracy and the Global Order: From the Modern State to Cosmopolitan Governance*, Stanford University Press, Palo Alto, CA, 1996; U. Beck, *What is Globalization?*, Polity Press, Cambridge, 2000), argue that globalization is in fact compatible with democracy. Globalization makes possible the extension of human rights to all countries, and cultural *métissage* promotes human understanding and a harmony not only of trade but also of ways of life. The global village can become a global civil society, traversed by a cosmopolitan *governance* or organized into a transnational state.

This is a left, liberal and humanistic version of the thesis that globalization helps democracy: here global society is viewed optimistically, as a process that can lead to the development of forms of world government.

(3) The position of capitalist democracy

Here we have the right-wing version of globalizing optimism. For example, in the view of Thomas Friedman (*The Lexus and the Olive Tree*, Anchor Books, London, 2000) the globalization of capital is in itself a globalization of democracy. This position has been carried to extremes, even to the point of caricature, by Francis Fukuyama (*The End of History and the Last Man*, Free Press, New York, 1992), who argues that the 'American way of life', that is, US hegemony, in itself represented the triumph of world democracy, and with that the end of history.

That is how the optimistic right-wing view of globalization conceives of the development of democracy.

(4)   The position of traditionalist conservatism

This brings us to the pessimistic right-wing view of the relationship between globalization and democracy. Particularly interesting
are the arguments of John Gray (*False Dawn: The Delusions of
Global Capitalism*, The New Press, New York, 1998), who maintains, first, that the decline in control by the nation-state leads to
anarchy and global instability, and, secondly, that the global spread
of the 'American way of life' unavoidably harms national identities
and destroys the self-determination of peoples, thereby creating
further instabilities. With this pessimistic position (carried to
extremes by Pat Buchanan, who sees globalization as producing
a hybridization of values also within the USA, and thus an assault
on American values) we also have the aggressive thesis of Samuel
Huntington (*The Clash of Civilizations and the Remaking of World
Order*, Simon & Schuster, New York, 1996), who offers the 'clash
of civilizations' as the solution to the difficulty of extending
democracy in globalization – the analysis is prescriptive and
warmongering.

So that gives us the fourth of our viewpoints – the right-wing
pessimistic position on the relationship between globalization and
democracy.

Having outlined these positions, it seems to us that, while each
of them has some value, we need to go further. Each of these positions, in fact, addresses the problem of the formation of the global
order back to front, so to speak – starting from its outcome. What
we need to do is to grasp the process of globalization (and, within
it, the relationship with democracy) from the point of view of the
dynamics that produce it. The methodological difference of *Empire*,
compared with the positions outlined here, is that it considers the
process of globalization not only in its final outcome, but also in
terms of its dynamics. *Dynamics that are basically determined by the
conflicts taking place within capitalist development.*

This brings us to the third basic thesis underpinning *Empire*,
following on the institutionalist thesis, which says that there is no
globalization without regulation, and the anti-nationalist thesis,
which sees sovereignty as being in a state of transition towards
new forms. The third thesis involves addressing these phenomena
from within the capital relation. This is the basic scientific claim
of *Empire*. Here we are obviously moving along paths mapped by

Marx. Naturally, this Marxian strategy is subjected to a new and creative experimentation, and to a sense of the originality of the situations that we are analysing. The class conflict within which we live, the experiences of power that we have, the practices of resistance and exodus that we live, and the very working activity that constitutes us, all these are *quite different* from what Marx experienced. The basic fundamental fact remains that *it is the struggle – that is, the social playing-out of the capital relation – that constitutes every political reality*.

Having said this, we need to consider one further element before moving on to discuss methodology. This is an element that marks our point of view as somewhat original. Our research arises out of the need to introduce a methodological variant that considers the process of imperial constitution not in its final outcome (i.e. as happens on both the right and the left every time that a teleological or ideological point of view is imposed), but in its dynamics. Dynamics that are essentially determined by the conflicts taking place within capitalist development and by the struggles which produce it. Thus our methodological variant is first and foremost *conflictual*: it implies an alternative (and the solution to that) for every position that emerges. There are some who consider the conflictual matrix as being in some way wrong, because it would imply a dialectical reasoning, built around rigid alternatives. The critics say that it would be better to have a multiversal schema of explanation. I do not believe that a conflictual point of view implies a monocausal and/or dialectical schema. However, as we proceed we shall have the possibility of verifying the extent to which the conflictual matrix can present itself in untimely terms. In the second place, the method (the methodological variant) that we employ is based on the relationship between material labour and immaterial labour, or rather on the process of *transition* from the one to the other. This is the social dimension that characterizes the ontological substrate on which our methodological variant operates. In the third place, the conflictual matrix, opening itself to the genealogy of the constituent processes, alternates moments of resistance and moments of expression of *potenza*.* Our method

* *Translator's note*: I have preferred to maintain here the Italian term *potenza*, but translate *potere* as 'power'. The distinction can be understood in the difference between the French *puissance* and *pouvoir*. Other authors have chosen to render them as power (lower case) and Power (upper case) or as 'power-to' and 'power-over'.

is always articulated within its ability to resist the objectivity of power and/or to express new realities, seen in terms of *potenza*. Fourthly and finally, what is being played out in our method is the very destiny of the social subjects and the multitudes: in fact it has to orient itself between the possibility of radical, revolutionary transformation and possible transient outcomes of flight: *here exodus is counterposed to revolution, but also implements it.*

Our scientific project is thus determined around the interplay of these alternatives. It is not a dialectical method; rather, it is a method that is open to verification by the event.

2

A Conversation about *Empire*

Between Antonio Negri and Danilo Zolo[*]

ZOLO   I have to confess that for a long time I have resisted invitations which have come to me from various quarters to debate *Empire*, the book which you and Michael Hardt published in the United States a few years ago and which has promoted, on both sides of the Atlantic, a debate of remarkable breadth and intensity. What held me back was a sense of impotence in the face of a work that is so broad, complex and ambitious. I overcame my hesitations by telling myself that after 11 September 2001 it would be irresponsible not to take seriously a book like *Empire*. It is a book which, whatever you think of it, invests substantial intellectual resources in an effort to contribute to the understanding of the world in which we live; which denounces the risks and atrocities of the present 'global order'; and which tries to suggest directions that could be followed to go beyond it. If for no other reasons than these, in my opinion *Empire* deserves the international success which it has enjoyed.

NEGRI   I thank you for your broadly positive view of the book and its international impact. The problem is that now, in addition

* First published in *Reset*, no. 73, September–October 2002, pp. 8–19.

to a certain quality of 'banality' that the book had right from the start (to me it seems almost like a film describing Empire, rather than a book), we have the problem that it is being overtaken by the course of events. The book's 'grand narrative' guaranteed its success and made it accessible to students on US campuses around the time of Seattle, and then in various other parts of the world, particularly in Germany. After the decade of the 1980s, after the defeat of the struggles and the triumph of *pensiero debole* ('weak thought'), something of a jolt was needed. *Empire* has given that jolt.

ZOLO   *Empire* is a major undertaking, not only in terms of its size and thematic scope, but also because its philosophical and theoretical-political syntax is very original. It is a syntax that trans-figures fundamental categories of Marxism, interpolating them with elements drawn from a broad and varied span of Western philosophical literature: classical, modern and contem-porary. In this transfiguration a prominent role is given to the post-structuralism of authors such as Gilles Deleuze, Jacques Derrida and, above all, Michel Foucault. My impression is that a careful and demanding reading of *Empire*, such as the book both deserves and invites, leads to interpretative results that are unavoidably controversial. Although its tone is often assertive and prescriptive, it is a book that risks transmitting more theo-retical uncertainties than certainties.

NEGRI   What you say about the philosophical categories under-pinning the book is correct. As to whether the book transmits more uncertainties than certainties, this idea appeals to me. With *Empire*, Michael Hardt and I had no intention of arriving at con-clusions: the fact of the matter is that the constitutive process of Empire is still largely open. What we wanted to make clear was the need for a change of register: the political philosophy of modernity (and, obviously, the institutions with which it inter-acted) has run its course. The theory that leads from Marsilius of Padova to Hobbes and from Althusius to Schmitt is finished. *Empire* is a new theoretical threshold.

ZOLO   Marx's philosophy and that of Foucault – to put it very summarily – are divergent theoretical vectors: Marxism argues for an organic, solidarity-based, egalitarian, disciplined society, whereas Foucault is an acute and radical critic of disciplinary power in the name of an anthropology that is individualistic and libertarian.

NEGRI   We have kept Foucault and Marx together. Or rather, in my case, I can say that I have 'rinsed my washing' in the Seine – in other words I created a hybrid between my workerist Marxism and the perspectives of French post-structuralism. I had already begun to do this during my years in prison (from 1979 to 1983), working on Spinoza, an excellent terrain of ontological encounter for this operation. Then, with Hardt in Paris, we deepened the analysis and immersed ourselves in that common 'aura' which, from the 1960s onwards, albeit unrecognized, linked workerism and post-structuralism, but also many tendencies in the broader area of subaltern studies and other post-colonial approaches. This was a crucial moment – for me at least – the moment when I realized that the phenomenon of Italian workerism was far from provincial. Spivak, publishing a collection of subaltern studies articles in the 1980s, bore direct witness to it; the influence of workerism was already recognized by Deleuze and Guattari in *Mille Plateaux*. Within this framework, Foucault's reading of Marx, which extends the genealogy of the processes of exploitation from the factory to the social realm, was fundamental for us. In our interpretation (unlike yours), Foucault is the creator of an anthropology which is certainly libertarian, but not individualistic; he is the constructor of a biopolitics within which what is being created is no longer the individual but a subject (and with how much singularity!). For our part, in Paris in the 1980s and 1990s, we already had a full awareness of having arrived in postmodernity. Thus we were in a new era, and we believed (as we still do) that Marx can be entirely integrated into the analytical methodologies of postmodernity. There is always a point at which the decision of what is new and strong breaks through: what a pleasure it was to be able to break with the pale derivations of modernity, with the likes of Rawls and Habermas . . . What a delight to recognize, along with Machiavelli (and all the others), that, *mutatis mutandis*, it is the class struggle that commands thought.

ZOLO   I have a second confession to make before we move on to discuss the central themes of *Empire*. It still makes me uneasy to be dealing with a treatise whose authors proclaim themselves to be 'communists' and who, moreover, say that they have taken Karl Marx's *Capital* as their expositional paradigm. Personally I have the greatest respect for what theoretical Marxism has been during the last century – albeit less respect for the experiences of 'real socialism' that took it as their basis – but these days I am not very inclined to look favourably on revisitings or 're-foundings' of Marxist philosophy, even when they are presented in critical and innovative forms. Personally, I settled my accounts with theoretical Marxism nearly thirty years ago – in fact I recall some particularly intense discussions with yourself – and I think I can claim to have done so seriously. I have taken my leave of Marxism because I am unable to share its three theoretical pillars: the dialectical philosophy of history, with its 'scientific laws' of development; the labour theory of value as the basis of the critique of the capitalist mode of production and as the premise of communist revolution; and the theory of the abolition of the state, with the accompanying rejection of the 'state of right' and of the doctrine of subjective rights. Your communism, despite the richness of its motivations, strikes me as being still rooted in the code of Marxist orthodoxy.

NEGRI   A lot has probably changed since our discussions of thirty years ago. However, if Marxism could be reduced to the three theoretical pillars that you mention, I myself would not be a Marxist (and I think I wouldn't have been so thirty years ago either). However, it seems to me that, along with the bath-water – more or less dirty, and sometimes downright filthy – you are also throwing out the baby. I take the opposite position – I want to recover Marxism. For me it is synonymous with modern materialism and is the summary and expression of a critical current that has traversed modernity, being continuously fought by it: the line that runs from Machiavelli through to Spinoza and Marx. For me, the recovery of Marxism, and its renewal, has the same strong meaning as the patristic apologetics of the first centuries in the history of Christianity: it is a 'return to principles', in Machiavelli's sense. Operating in this direction means moving forward on some of the basic points of Marxist theory: it means going against the dialectics of history and building a non-teleological theory of class struggle; going beyond the labour theory of value, to analyse valorization in terms of a general intellect, in the age of the real (and fully achieved) subsumption of society within capital; and, as regards the theory of the state, it means grasping sovereignty (the point of coincidence of the economic and the political) as the central moment in the exercise of exploitation, and also of mystification and of the destruction of subjective rights. Marx never wrote the book he proposed to write, on class struggles. Nor, more particularly, did he write the book on the state. In effect, the book on the state, which is missing from *Capital*, could only have been written when the space of sovereignty had become as large as the world, and it was therefore possible to confront Empire with the multitude. The nation-state, which was all that Marx could have talked about, was a hotch-potch of the Middle Ages and modernity which capitalist development itself could only handle with difficulty. Only a proletariat that was international and internationalist could have posed the problem of the state.

ZOLO The part of *Empire* which I find most successful, and which in my opinion demands fresh 'strategic' thinking about the structure and the functions of the processes of global integration, is the part which deals with the notion of 'Empire' itself. As we know, you and Hardt think that the new 'world order' imposed by globalization has led to the disappearance of the Westphalian system of sovereign states. National states no longer exist, except in bloodless formal structures that still survive within juridical systems and international institutions. The world is no longer governed by state-political systems; it is governed by a single structure of power which is not analogous in any meaningful sense with the modern state of European origin. It is a decentred and deterritorialized political system, which develops outside the frame of ethnic–national traditions and values, and whose political and normative essence is cosmopolitan universalism. For these reasons you think that 'Empire' is the most appropriate name for this new type of global power . . .

NEGRI I should add that we are not at all nostalgic for the nation-state. Moreover, we believe that this development, both real and conceptual, which you have summed up very well, has been driven by a motor which is that of working-class struggles, anti-colonial struggles and, latterly, the struggles against the social-ist management of capital – the struggles for freedom – in the countries of 'real socialism'. These were the main movements of the last third of the twentieth century.

ZOLO   Therefore it would be mistaken to think that the Empire – or its central and expansive nucleus – consists of the United States and its closest Western allies. You and Hardt say forcefully in your book that neither the United States nor any other national state 'currently constitutes the centre of an imperialist project'. According to you, the global Empire is therefore something quite different from classic imperialism, and it would be a serious theoretical error to confuse the one with the other. Do I interpret you correctly?

NEGRI   Your interpretation is correct. Let me add that, in par-ticular at Porto Alegre, one had a measure of how dangerous it might be if the building of the 'movement of movements' were to base itself on nation-states. Equivocal forms of nationalism and populism would end up being taken on board by the *No Global* movement. Anti-Americanism and a belief in the nation-state nearly always go hand in hand: this is the kind of messy thinking that we have inherited from Third-Worldist socialism – which has always seemed to me as serious a diversion as that of Soviet Marxism.

ZOLO   This is a very delicate point and one that has raised numer-ous reservations, some of which I share. In your book, Empire seems to evaporate into a kind of 'category of the spirit': like God, it is present in every place, since it coincides with the new dimen-sion of globality. But one could object that if everything is im-perial then nothing is imperial. How are we to identify the supra-national subjects who are the bearers of the imperial inter-ests or aspirations, in order to make them the object of a global struggle? Against whom are we to turn our anti-imperialistic cri-tique and resistance, if states and their political forces are not the things that we should be targeting? Is this an Empire that does not exercise a political–military power? Does it only express itself through instruments of economic – or, at most, ideological – constraint?

NEGRI   The process of imperial constitution is under way. The instruments which global capital is already, palpably, setting into operation are tending towards such a limit: these instruments are sovereign, economic, military, cultural, and so on. Now, it is beyond doubt that in this phase Empire is marked by a great tension between an institutional *non-place* and the series of global instruments (global, but partial from the point of view of sovereignty) used by collective capital. You are right to say that if everything is imperial then nothing is imperial. However, following the example of Polybius, we identify some places or forms of imperial government: the monarchic function that the government of the United States, the G8 and other monetary and commercial institutions have assigned themselves; the aristocratic power of the multinationals as they extend their networks over the global market. The global movement of the multitude (as it emerged post-Seattle) certainly had many doubts about how to identify, within the continuous creation of poverty and exclusion, within the violent and bellicose response to their protest, the points against which to mobilize critique and resistance. However, these points are very real, and can be identified in the distortion of economic development, in the destruction of planet Earth, and in the increasingly massive attempts to appropriate all things between earth and the ether that are 'common' to humanity. The paradox (and the drama) of our present moment is that Empire will only succeed in forming its structures by *responding* to the struggles of the multitude: but all this, in the manner of Machiavelli, is a process of clashes between powers. We are only at the beginning of a new 'Thirty Years War' – that was how long it took the modern state to formalize its birth.

ZOLO   You maintain that the 'imperial constitution' is distinguished from the state constitution by its functions. Imperial sovereignty does not seek the inclusion and political–territorial assimilation of subordinated countries or peoples, as was the characteristic of imperialism and state-based colonialism in the 1800s and 1900s. The new imperial command exercises itself via political institutions and juridical apparatuses whose objective is basically the guarantee of global order, in other words of a 'stable and universal peace' for the normal operation of the market economy. At various times you talk about functions of 'international policing', and even about judicial functions carried out by Empire. In general I agree, but I have one important reservation: if it is not the political–military apparatuses of the major Western powers – and, first and foremost, the United States – that exercise these imperial functions, then who does?

NEGRI   I do not find it strange that Empire presents itself as guaranteeing world order through a stable and universal peace, using all the political-military means that it has at its disposal. Bush and his associates make these declarations of peace, and every day they carry out acts of war. However, we should not confuse Bush and the political–military apparatuses that he employs with the government of Empire. It seems to me, rather, that the present ideology and *imperialist* practice of the Bush government is fast putting itself on a collision course with the capitalist forces which, at world-wide level, are working for Empire. The situation is completely open. I expect that later in this conversation we shall return to the issue of war as a specific form of imperial control: for the moment I would just like to emphasize that, at the level of Empire, the war function and the policing function are increasingly merging. However, apart from some specific points that I shall go into later, I feel I should again stress that anti-Americanism is a weak and mystifying way of proceeding in the present phase of critical definition of the new world constitution. Anti-Americanism confuses the American people with the American state; it does not realize that the US operates within a world market, in the same way as Italy or South Africa, and that Bush's politics are very minoritarian among the world-wide aristocracies of multinational capitalism. Anti-Americanism is a dangerous state of mind, an ideology which mystifies the data supplied by analysis and which fails to deal adequately with the responsibilities of collective capital. We need to distance ourselves from it, just as much as we would distance ourselves from the pro-Americanism of the films of Alberto Sordi.

ZOLO   It is not a marginal circumstance, you claim, that the imperial juridical order is basically engaged in a juridical function, or a quasi-judicial arbitration. Imperial power is directly invoked by its subjects for its ability to resolve conflicts from a universal (i.e. impartial and neutral) point of view. And it is significant – as you claim perceptively in your book – that, after a long period of eclipse, during the past decade we have seen a resurgence of the doctrine of *bellum iustum* ('just war'), in other words a medieval doctrine which is typically universalistic and imperial. Is that right? I fully agree with this analysis, not least because it chimes with positions which I was putting forward years ago, particularly in my *Cosmopolis* [Feltrinelli, Milan, 1995]. But, I repeat, in my opinion the analysis is only meaningful if the 'imperial constitution' is conceived of as a political constitution. And in my view there can be absolutely no doubt that the United States – in other words, the cognitive, communicational, economic, political and military powers that are concentrated within the geopolitical space of the American superpower – is today the driving motor of this global strategic plan, whether you call it 'hegemonic', as I would prefer, or 'imperial' as you prefer, or whatever.

NEGRI   I do not agree. Also I really do not understand how you (who have shown us in your writings, from *Cosmopolis* through to *Chi dice umanità* [Einaudi, Turin, 2000], how much the political and juridical categories of modernity have been not only abused but also trodden underfoot) can propose a definition of the present processes of government of the world market that is still based on the modernist categories of imperialism. Here it is my turn to ask a question: what does it mean to talk about a potestative capacity of the state in the face of the *lex mercatoria*, in other words that substantive modification of international private law that sees not nation-states but law firms acting as legislators? (I could ask a dozen more questions on this point, but I hope we can avoid them.) And as for international public law: is it not pitiful to watch the pathetic attempts to relaunch the United Nations in this situation? The fact is that speaking of the United States as the driving motor of a global imperialist strategic project brings with it every kind of contradiction, particularly if one wishes to reserve for the government of the United States an exclusive capacity for command (as is implicit in modernity's theories of national sovereignty and imperialism).

ZOLO   In my view, the fact that the command power and the influence of the United States are radiating throughout the entire world, to the point of becoming a *global power*, as proclaimed in the State Department's recent *Quadrennial Defense Review Report*, does not contradict the fact that this power is territorial and culturally based in the United States, and that it can be identified with the American superpower also at the symbolic level.

NEGRI   I do not deny that the United States is a *global power*. The point is that American power itself is subject to (or at least constrained into dialogue and/or contestation with) economic and political structures which are other than it. The terrorist attack of 11 September 2001 was, among other things, also the demonstration of a state of civil war between forces wishing to be structurally represented in the imperial constitution. The people who destroyed the Twin Towers were those same 'condottieri' of the mercenary armies who have been hired in order to defend oil interests in the Middle East. They have nothing to do with the multitudes: they are elements internal to the imperial structure in the process of its becoming. One should absolutely not underestimate the civil war that is being pursued at the imperial level. To me it seems that we can say that American leadership is deeply weakened precisely by the imperialist tendencies which it sometimes expresses. It is obvious that these tendencies are not accepted in the Arab world any more than in the European world or in the socialist world – not to mention that 'other continent' known as China. The overweening military power of the United States is, as we know, largely neutralized by the impossibility of using its nuclear arsenal. And this is good news. From the monetary point of view, the United States is increasingly exposed and weakened on the financial markets: and this is also excellent news. In short, in all probability the United States will soon be forced to stop being imperialist and recognize itself as being within Empire.

ZOLO   There is a second aspect of your theory of Empire on which I have doubts. It is an aspect which I attribute to the implicit 'ontology' (the term is yours) that acts as metaphysical counterpoint to your analyses: the dialectics of history, in the terms characteristic of Hegelian Marxism and Leninism. In your view, the global Empire is a positive transcendence of the Westphalian system of sovereign states. Having put an end to states and their nationalism, the Empire has also put an end to classical colonialism and imperialism, opening the way to a cosmopolitan perspective that is to be welcomed. Any attempt to revive the nation-state in opposition to the present imperial constitution of the world should be seen as a 'false and harmful' ideology. The *no global* philosophy and all forms of environmental action and localism should thus be rejected as positions that are primitive and anti-dialectical and, in short, reactionary.

NEGRI   I don't think that these are fair accusations. As anyone knows who has read the book (as you obviously have), we entertain no dialectic but only the class struggle. It is the class struggle (a *dispositif* very much *à la Machiavelli*, which is open, non-determined, non-teleological and risky) that lies at the basis of our method. Here there is nothing of the dialectical, unless you extend that term to mean any analytical approach to historical development. Our narrative deals with a *telos* that is concrete – it deals with risk and with mankind's struggle against exploitation, so as to make life joyous and to remove the pain. Our political problem is thus that of proposing a space which is adequate to embrace all the struggles that start from below. In this framework there is no place for nostalgia and for the defence of the nation-state, of that absolute barbarism which was represented in Verdun, and in the bombing of Dresden, and in Hiroshima, and also (if I may say so) in Auschwitz. I do not know how one can still consider the nation-state as anything less than a false and harmful ideology. On the other hand, the networks of the movement of movements, like everything that happens freely in this world, are poliverse: they intersect with each other, and thus they have no difficulty in constructing, as indeed they have constructed, a unitary movement. Every attempt to prevent this unification and the consequent acknowledgement of *common* objectives is reactionary; in fact it expresses operations that are sectarian and hostile. The *No Global* philosophy and the movement of Seattle are internationalist and global.

ZOLO   The communists, you say, are by vocation universalist, cosmopolitan and 'catholic': their horizon is that of the whole of humanity, of 'generic human nature', as Marx would say. Remember that in the last century the working masses always aimed for an internationalization of political and social relations. For this reason you maintain that the 'global' powers of Empire must be controlled, but not demolished: the imperial constitution should be preserved and directed to other ends. From the point of view of the transition to a communist society, the construction of the Empire is 'a step forward': the Empire, you write, 'is better than what came before it' because 'it eliminates the cruel regimes of modern power' and 'offers enormous possibilities for creation and liberation'. I fail to share this dialectical optimism, which plainly has a Hegelian and Marxist ancestry.

NEGRI   I really wouldn't say that our position expresses dialectical optimism. Furthermore, it is clear that you are dead set on the term 'dialectical': anything you don't like becomes 'dialectical'. So may I suggest an author who is certainly not dialectical but who is certainly capable of looking ahead: Spinoza. Here, in his philosophy, the optimism has absolutely nothing to do with Hegel: it has to do with freedom and the joy of freeing oneself from slavery . . . Now, these are the multitude, i.e. a multiplicity of singularities, already hybridized or *métissés*, capable of immaterial and intellectual labour, with an enormous *potenza* for freedom. This is not dialectics but sociological, factual and to-the-point analysis – of the transformations taking place in labour, of its organization and of the political subjectivity which derives from that. I cannot imagine that, instead of global mobility and a flexibility in the time of life and of labour, you prefer the archaic peasant-based or artisanal traditions, embodied in the realm of non-effectual myth. Or the misery of the mass worker, tied to the assembly line. The expansion of life prospects and the intellectual and moral enrichment of workers seem to me to be good things. It is here that Empire can be seen as good *in itself*.

ZOLO   The post-colonial analyses convince me more – I am thinking in particular of the 'subaltern studies' people – inasmuch as they point to the continuity between classic colonialism and the present processes of hegemonic globalization. Today, after the parenthesis of the Cold War and the ephemeral liberation of colonized countries from their direct political subjection to the European powers, the West is once again engaged in a strategy of control, military occupation, commercial invasion and 'civilizing' of the non-Western world. It is precisely against this strategy that we see the bloody and impotent response of global terrorism, which, not accidentally, chooses to target almost exclusively the United States.

NEGRI   I don't think I can agree with you here. Certainly there is a thread of continuity between classic colonialism and the present processes of imperial globalization. But I would be very cautious about calling the liberation of colonial countries ephemeral, and about thinking that the geopolitical status quo has not been radically altered. The First, Second and Third Worlds have modified their positioning, not superficially but fundamentally: they have now become a mixture – you find the First World in deepest Africa and in the republics of Central Asia, just as you find the Third World in big European or American cities. If you look at all this from a spatial point of view, the situation, albeit modified, presents itself statically; but if you look at these same phenomena, these dislocations, from the point of view of their intensity, then you will be able to see (and this is very much what 'subaltern studies' is saying) the transformative potential of these processes, and the fact that they are threatening and global in extent. In this perspective, whereas global terrorism is part of the 'civil war' for imperial leadership, the movements of resistance and exodus are actually the real new threat for the global capitalist order.

ZOLO   In my opinion it is rather *against* Empire that one should be directing the struggle, taking a stand against its global expansionism and world-political ideology. I do not hanker nostalgically (as communitarian republicanism does) after a return to eighteenth-century nation-states, even though I am not at all convinced that nation-states are now merely historical leftovers. I share the view of Ulrich Beck, who says that they are now transforming themselves into 'transnational' states, whose civil society is traversed by a quantity of multinational agencies and institutions such as big economic corporations, the financial markets, information and communication technologies, the culture industry and so on. It is clear, in my view, that states are redefining their functions, focusing above all on issues of security and public order, as has been argued by Pierre Bourdieu and Loïc Wacquant. According to Thomas Mathiesen, we are in a transition from the 'panoptic' state to the 'synoptic' state, thanks to the huge possibilities of control offered by the new technologies and by the electronic data banks that are being set up unbeknownst to the general public. But states are a long way from becoming 'extinct'. In fact, some of them are getting a lot stronger.

NEGRI   I agree broadly with what you are saying, and I respect the literature that you cite. I too believe that nation-states have not disappeared: to me this seems obvious. It also seems obvious to me that the articulation of functions of universal domination and internal public order is also coming to be a specialist activity of the nation-state (maintaining their *continuum*). But saying that many functions of the nation-state still survive is not the same as saying that nation-states are tendentially going to continue to exist, or that they will become stronger. On the contrary, even the associations of nation-states, traversed as they might be by transnational *dispositifs* (*à la* Beck), are, in my view, to be seen within the processes of hierarchization and specialization of Empire. I mean that the question of the universal guarantee of (global) order has by now been posed in terms that are *irreversible*. The epochal transition is now a given. It is within this flow and in the face of this problem that theoretical and political choices must be characterized.

ZOLO   My opinion is rather that it we should be thinking of – and operating via – new forms of global equilibrium, in the name of a multipolar regionalism capable of balancing and then reducing and defeating the aggressive strategic unilateralism of the imperial power of the United States. And a Europe freed from the suffocating Atlantic embrace – a Europe that was less Western and more Mediterranean and 'oriental' – could fulfil an important function in this sense. This is also the direction in which the Chinese-Confucian bloc is quietly operating in south-east and north-east Asia.

NEGRI   New forms of global organization, articulated on the basis of multipolar regionalism, are much to be wished for. Furthermore, this is what is already happening within the world market, in the process that leads to the construction of imperial sovereignty. I fail to understand what this process is preferable to, since it is exactly what is already happening. If anything, the problem is how to take action, from any one of the points of the Empire, in order to open scenarios of global destabilization. It is only within this framework that a transformation of the rules of domination and exploitation could become possible. It is obvious, therefore, that I do not accept the notion of 'equilibrium', which is a fruit of other philosophical epochs. Whether organized in regional terms or not, what we always have is not equilibrium but hierarchy, not multipolarity but multifunctionality.

ZOLO   I would add that a multipolar equilibrium is the precondition for international law to be able to ensure even a minimal function of containment of the more destructive consequences of modern war.

NEGRI   What you say seems entirely true: Empire and international law negate each other. But this was the observation that was our starting point. This is an irreversible condition. Hence my deep scepticism regarding the sticking-plaster politics of UN internationalism. There is a huge literature (which you yourself have studied) on reviving the United Nations, and on the building of a global 'civil society' that could take on the role of interlocutor with the sovereign in the new global ordering. Even the World Bank has expressed views along these lines. And yet the attempts to reactivate a participative and normative 'international' (in the Westphalian sense) system have come to nothing. Even when it goes towards meeting the subjective rights of citizens and nations, of groups and associations (for instance with the setting up of the big international courts), legal reformism has had the upper hand over classic international law.

ZOLO   After 11 September the situation of international imbalance has been aggravated further. What we now have is a hegemonic strategy of permanent war, without territorial borders, without time limits, in large part secret, and more than ever incapable of being controlled on the basis of international law. Today as never before, Western political-military élites seem to realize that in order to guarantee the security and well-being of the industrialized countries it is necessary to exercise a growing military pressure over the entire world.

NEGRI   I see the necessity of resisting a capitalism which is becoming increasingly parasitic and predatory, whose legitimation (both in itself and through the imperial and statal instruments with which it is identified) is becoming completely bellicose. As Foucault and Deleuze showed, we have moved from the disciplinary regimes (over individuals) of classical capitalism to the regimes of control (over populations) of mature capitalism. Today that type of legitimation has war built in. Poverty and marginalization are thus not only maintained, but also continuously recreated through imperial wars. New borders, both territorial and racial, are being created by imperial war. My only problem in all this is to understand what is the resistance – to war, poverty and exploitation – that can be enacted against it. Your geography of domination, for all that may be correct about it, has to be opposed by a topology of resistance: from this point of view *subcomandante* Marcos is more important than the entire American 'revolution in military affairs'. What interests me is David facing Goliath, facing every imperial Goliath: as the military would say, 'asymmetrical resistance'. And it is for this reason that the global picture of resistance is becoming powerful: because, despite the relentless and continuous operation of enclosure that the imperial armadas produce, there are always liberated spaces within globalization – holes and folds through which an exodus of resistance can take place.

ZOLO   I suggest that we conclude our discussion with one final question, namely that of the subject or subjects of what, for you and Hardt, should be a revolution *within* Empire. I use the term 'revolution' in all its anthropological fullness, because this is the meaning that seems to be implied by your communist project. You are thinking, in classic terms, of a transformation of the world that is not only political, but also ethical and cultural.

NEGRI   In addition to envisioning revolution in ethical and political terms, we also conceive of it in terms of deep anthropological modification: of *métissage* and continuous hybridization of populations, of biopolitical metamorphosis. The first terrain of struggle is, from this point of view, the universal right to move, work and learn over the entire surface of the globe. Thus revolution, as we see it, is not only within Empire but also *through* Empire. It is not something which is fought against some implausible Winter Palace, but something which extends against all the central and peripheral structures of power, in order to empty them and subtract the capacity of production from capital.

ZOLO   The subject of this revolution *within* Empire is what you choose to call the 'multitude'. I say 'choose to call' with critical intent: 'multitude' is, in my opinion, a rather slippery concept, the least fortunate term in the entire conceptual arsenal of *Empire*. Nowhere in your book do you offer an analytical definition of it – based on political–sociological categories – which might help the reader to identify this collective subject within given socio-political contexts. Instead of analysis, in many parts of the book you launch into high-sounding phrases about the '*potenza* of the multitude' – its power 'to be, to love, to transform and to create' – and its 'desire' for emancipation. I fear that here you follow in the footsteps of Marxist messianism and its grandiose political simplifications. The 'multitude' appears to me like some vague reincarnation of the nineteenth-century proletariat, the class that Marx elevated to the status of demiurge of history. I say this with bitterness and without the slightest irony.

NEGRI   You are right to criticize the lack of a sufficiently analytical definition of the concept of multitude in *Empire*. I am happy to make a self-criticism here, not least because Michael Hardt and I are doing a lot of work on this question. I believe, however, that the concept of multitude in the book can be understood within at least three perspectives. The first is polemical in relation to the two definitions that have been given of the populations inserted within the procedures of sovereignty in the age of modernity: 'people' and 'mass'. In our view, the multitude is a *multiplicity* of singularities which cannot in any sense find a representative *unity*. The 'people', on the one hand, is an artificial unity that the modern state requires as the basis of the fiction of legitimation; 'mass', on the other hand, is a concept which realist sociology assumes as the basis of the capitalist mode of production (in both the liberal and the socialist aspect of capital management), and which in any event is an undifferentiated unity. For us, on the other hand, men are singularities, a multitude of singularities. A second meaning of multitude derives from the fact that we oppose it to 'class'. In present-day sociology of labour, the worker presents himself increasingly as the bearer of immaterial capacities of production. The worker reappropriates to himself the instrument of labour. In immaterial productive labour the instrument is the brain (so this brings us to the end of the Hegelian dialectics of the instrument of labour). This singular capacity of labour is what constitutes the workers as multitude rather than as class. Here, consequently, we have a third terrain of definition, the more specifically political one. We see the multitude as a political *potenza* which is *sui generis*: it is in relation to this, in other words in relation to a multitude of singularities, that the new political categories have to be defined. We think that these new political categories must be identified via the analysis of the *common* rather than through the hypostasis of unity. But here is not the place to take this analysis further: I say this with much irony.

ZOLO   In my opinion, your book leaves unresolved the problem of the new spaces and new subjects of global contestation – of the 'new militants', to use Marco Revelli's term. Your indications go in the direction of a recovery of political struggle at a global level, now that engagement in the political arenas of the nation-state has lost meaning and efficacy. But it seems to me that you have not paid sufficient attention to the question, which Massimo Cacciari recently highlighted in his *Duemilauno: Politica e futuro* [with G. Bettin, Feltrinelli, Milan 2001], of the 'depoliticization of the world' by the big powers of technology and the economy. On the contrary, there are pages of your book that seem animated by a thorough-going technological and industrialistic fervour – labouristic, one could say – in relation to the *network society*, to use Manuel Castells' term. It is as if you see the technological and digital revolution as the vector of an imminent communist revolution.

NEGRI   We are very attentive to the revolution in digital technology – obviously, since we remain Marxists and we believe that, although the law of value no longer functions as a law capable of measuring the development of capitalism, work is and remains part of the dignity of the human beings and the substance of their history. The technological and digital revolution opens up the possibility of new spaces of liberation. At the same time, it is also bringing into being new forms of slavery. But *the reappropriation of the instrument* of labour on the part of the worker, the concentration of valorization in the *cooperation* of cognitive workers, the extension of knowledge and the importance of science in the processes of production, all these [factors] bring about new material conditions which must be considered to be favourable to the prospects of transformation. The problem of political organization now has to pay heed to *this* multitude, just as the development of the trade union or the socialist party had to pay heed to the different and consecutive figures of the proletariat. The depoliticization of the world by the big powers is not only a negative operation, when its effect is to remove and/or unmask old powers and forms of representation which no longer have any basis in reality.

ZOLO In my view, your adoption of the term 'multitude' is also a profession of radical political anti-individualism. *Empire* represents an almost complete shift away from the European liberal–democratic tradition. I fear that this is the point that divides us most.

NEGRI I agree that the term multitude (and what it contains) represents a position of radical political anti-individualism. *Empire* implies the refusal of the tradition of possessive individualism. But I do not believe that this involves the abandonment of the European liberal–democratic tradition, in the sense that, with the concept of multitude, what we are seeking is, *à la* Spinoza, an 'absolute democracy'. Our problem, as it was also Spinoza's, is not the putting together of isolated individ-uals, but rather that of constructing, in cooperative fashion, forms and instruments of common-ness which lead to the (ontological) acknowledgement of the common. From air to water, right through to the digital economy and its networks, that is the terrain on which freedom is extended: how is the common to be organized?

ZOLO I also find unsatisfactory – although I recognize the courage and the theoretical originality that you display in attempting to deal with topics that I consider very difficult – your suggestions of 'nomadism' and *'métissage'* as instruments for a world-political struggle to be conducted within the parasitic chrysalis of Empire. Nomadism and *métissage* – you claim – are the weapons to be used against enslavement to reactionary ideologies such as nation, ethnicity, people and race. 'Multitude' becomes a powerful concept thanks to its capacity for circulation, for 'navigation', for contamination. I tend to think that here you underestimate the fact that nomadism, *métissage* and cultural creolization are effects of the great migratory flows created by the growing international imbalances of power and wealth. Serge Latouche has suggested that these effects of 'deculturation', 'deterritorialization' and 'planetary uprooting' can be read as a real failure of the project of modernization, as a setback to its Promethean universalism.

NEGRI I am very pleased you are enthusiastic, if I understand you correctly, about the effectiveness of our theses on *métissage* and nomadism. But then your judgement tips towards pessimism. I have often read what Serge Latouche has to say on these matters. I have to say, if I do not accept his position, this is not because I disagree with much of what he says, but simply because his position is burdened with an all-devouring catastrophism. I do not understand why people's flight through migration and the search for hope by so many peoples around the world should be derided as 'Promethean universalism'. I do not believe that these migrants are only trying to escape poverty; I believe that they are also seeking freedom, knowledge and wealth. Desire is a constructive *potenza* and is particularly powerful when it is implanted in poverty: *poverty*, in fact, is not simply misery, but is also the *possibility* of very many things, which desire indicates and which labour produces. The migrant has the dignity of the person who seeks after truth, production, and happiness. And this is the strength that breaks the enemy's capacity to isolate and exploit, and which removes, together with the supposed Prometheanism, every heroic and/or theological tendency from the behaviour of the poor and the subversive. If anything, the Prometheanism of poor people, of the migrants, is the salt of the Earth, and the world really is changed by nomadism and *métissage.*

ZOLO   Finally I would like to ask you – even though I realize that it's a hard question to answer – what are the institutional forms and normative modalities of this thing that you call 'counter-Empire', in other words the 'alternative political organization of global flows and exchanges'? It is this political organization which, you claim, the 'creative forces of the multitude are autonomously capable of constructing'. What do you mean, concretely? All I have been able to infer from a close reading of your book is that, either way, it will have to be an imperial political form. This, in my view, is not very satisfactory at either the theoretical or the political level. But, above all, it is symptomatic of your holding to a position that is very reminiscent of the Marxist theory of the 'extinction of the state'. The Empire is the institutional shell within which states and their juridical orderings will be dissolved, 'will fall asleep' (*otmira-nie*), as Lenin said. Here too, in line with Marxist orthodoxy – from *The Jewish Question* onwards – the entire doctrine of the 'state of right' [*stato di diritto*] and of the protection of fundamental freedoms is ignored in your book, together with themes such as respect for political minorities and the self-determination of peoples. In your book, the power of the 'multitude' is thought of as an unlimited, global and permanent constituent energy: a collective energy that expresses 'generative *potenza*, desire and love'.

NEGRI   You have certainly studied 'the abolition of the state' in the Marxist classics more than I have, because I have been more concerned with problems of transition. If I tell you that I find all that stuff ridiculous, I think that would meet only with your approval. But I also think that the entire doctrine of the 'state of right' has become rather senile, and we need to set hands on your 'substance of freedom' if we don't want to end up carrying on philosophizing in a void of meaning. And, as to what the multitude will do against the Empire, I place all my trust in what the militants of the global movements think and do. Believe me, they are much more intelligent and capable than we were, and they are starting young.

3

LESSON 1

On Historical Method: Causality and Periodization

In the Preface we stressed the internal, endogenous perspective of imperial development. And we also stated that, determining this perspective, we would have to take as our starting point the analysis of *the concept of capital*. Now, the concept of capital that we use is not defined in an objective and static way, but is rather premised on the idea of a relationship, an inter-relation: in other words, capital and capitalism are *categories of a relationship*, of a relation which embraces both those who command and those who obey, those who exploit and those who are exploited, those who order and those who obey orders, those who subordinate and those who are subordinated. If we take this relationship as our starting point, it means that we have to understand that globalization is not a linear expansion of the market – for example, one which sweeps away the nation-state. What we have to realize is that nowadays the nation-state is incapable of exercising control over the capital relationship. In other words: today the nation-state is incapable of controlling the mechanisms of reproduction of society in capital's interests, and this is because the working-class struggles within the nation-state, and the anti-imperialist and anti-colonial struggles that have been conducted all over the world, and also the struggles for freedom against 'real socialism' – all these struggles now make it impossible for the nation-state to function as a point of equilibrium and as a sovereign guarantee of capitalist development.

The concept of capital is a concept of a social relationship. As such, this relationship needs to be regulated in such a way that the reproduction of society preserves capitalist proportions, or, to put it in more precise terms, allows for the reproduction of the capacity of command by capital; consequently the capitalist reproduction of society must be a reproduction in which the system can recognize itself, from phase to phase, as a whole and as an objective. Sovereignty is control over the reproduction of capital, and thus it is command over the proportions of the relations of force (workers and bosses, proletariat and bourgeoisie, the multitudes and imperial monarchy) that constitute it. In modernity, sovereignty resides in the nation-state. In postmodernity, sovereignty resides elsewhere (probably in Empire). Now, it is precisely at the level of the nation-state of the developed capitalist countries that we can identify the occurrence of a *first rupture* which forced sovereignty to locate itself elsewhere. This rupture happened in the post-1968 period. A new epoch was defined between 1971 (with the ending of the fixed parity of the dollar, i.e. the dollar-gold equivalent) and 1973, with the first big oil crisis and the limitation treaty for nuclear weapons (the ABM Treaty of 1972). This was precisely the moment of recognition of the impossibility of guaranteeing capitalist development through the instruments of domestic sovereign regulation, in other words, of controlling the capital relation from within the space of individual nation-states. The workers' pressure on wages, along with the ensuing inflationary processes of the early 1970s, blocked the possibility of the nation-state exercising control over a national space that was being racked by struggles, and of recomposing it for development. This was the phase which saw the emergence of the first forms of supra-national command in the true sense. They were the first ones not in chronological terms but because, in a new and original form, they began to take sovereignty away from the nation-state, not only in Europe but also in the USA. For instance, a series of instruments supportive of capitalist development – instruments which had been set up at the end of the Second World War (the World Bank, International Monetary Fund and the like) and which, during the Cold War, had assumed functions of internal regulation – were then transformed into instruments for the general control of development. These bodies become not only projections of American power (the so-called 'Washington Consensus') but also a location of supra-national equilibrium and of regulation of world-wide development.

Here we have described a historical situation of transformation, between modernity and postmodernity: let us now try to add to this description a sense of the endogenous causality of the process.

A *second element* characterizing the new situation is the end (another eminently causal element) of the imperialist phase of capitalist development. This also occurred during the 1960s and the 1970s, and it is obviously an element of major importance. However, here we should be clear that there is a conceptual difference between Empire and imperialism: it is a major difference. By imperialism we mean the expansive process of the power of the nation-state through policies of export of capital, export of labour power and constitution-occupation of areas of influence. Obviously, within imperialism we also include subspecies such as the institutions of colonialism. The major European nation-states develop (and determine capitalist development) through imperialist expansion.

Now, in the 1960s and 1970s the colonial–imperialist equilibrium that had been established in the preceding centuries was driven into serious crisis by a movement of extraordinary breadth, which shattered the imperialist and colonial system. This movement had its peak in the liberation struggle in Vietnam, a central political moment in a process that was general and *irreversible*. This was a further element determining the impossibility of the nation-state using force to achieve expansionist ends. As a consequence it also brought about major imbalances in the internal relationships of domination within the central nation-states. It drove the problems of control and reproduction of the capitalist system/society towards other places which were no longer those of the unilateral command of the nation-state, either within or without. We use the term Empire to refer to this *non-place* where the sovereignty that guarantees capitalist development at the world-wide level is concentrated.

The *third element* that needs to be taken into account is the end of the Second World, that is, the world of 'real' or 'actually existing' socialism. Indeed, one can also interpret the pressure to achieve freedom and the repeated attempts to overcome the 'Stalinist dictatorship for development' as phenomena related to basic changes taking place in the mode of production. In fact, many commentators now *define the crisis of the Soviet system by relating it to the transition from Fordism to post-Fordism*. Simplifying this position greatly, one could say that the new forms of producing, immaterial labour, and the personal computer and the degree of freedom that it implies, created a major crisis in a system as rigid as the Soviet one. That said, it should be added that here we find another essential phenomenon for explaining the inability of capitalist domination to control its own development. In the form of socialist management of capital, it clashes with the freedom that the development of labour, in the shift from Fordism to post-Fordism and from the hegemony of material labour to that of immaterial labour, had placed at the heart of production. In the spaces of the Russian nation-state and of the Soviet imperialist system, it was the demand for freedom that put sovereignty into crisis. A freedom that was material and biopolitical: how can we forget those epic scenes of nomadism and the flight of workers that brought masses of workers from East Germany to the West, via Hungary and Austria and bypassing the Wall! In this case it was mobility that brought down tyranny.

Therefore, once again, we find that it is struggles, *within* and *against* capitalist command, that make history and, in particular, explode the control-space of the nation-state, and drive towards the constitution of Empire.

Let us start by asking ourselves *where this type of endogenous methodology comes from*, which takes the struggles of the pro-letariat as the driving motor of development. For my part, the answer is: *from Italian workerism (operaismo)*, in other words, from that renewed Marxism which from the late 1950s through to the definitive crisis and dismantling of the international communist movement has built an interpretation of Marxism which made it possible to develop the category of 'the autonomy of the working class'. As we know, in *Capital* the concept of working class is formed as a political refinement of the concept of labour power. As for labour power, it is the social figure of the economic concept of variable capital. Labour power and variable capital were therefore concepts which were formed *within* capital. It is clear that capital has had the huge historical function of constructing labour power, but this function was given, both in classical economics and also, partially, in its critique, within a relation of capital as a situation and determination that were entirely static. The concept of working class was, in this framework, also constructed in static terms, as a mechanical projection of labour power, and hence, once again, as a figure internal to capital. Soviet state socialism used this figure of the working class within its disciplinary regime. In the Marxist tradition it was therefore impossible to represent the movement of the working class as an *independent variable*, independent of the capital relation; whereas, on the contrary, the historical analyses that superimposed themselves on the critique of political economy gave ample opportunities to identify movements of the working class against capital which constructed material plans, strategies, teleologies and utopias, often with powerful results. So we had to turn Marx's interpretation on its head and reverse the picture: *the working class, through its struggles, was the motor of all development.* The working class was defined by its subjective being, by its ability to reveal itself as event and by its ability to dispose itself as social constitution.

It is Mario Tronti who takes the credit for having formalized, in his *Operai e capitale* [*Workers and Capital*], these theoretical hypotheses that have provided such powerful analytical tools for so many researchers. Obviously, thinking in terms of a spontaneity within the movements of the class, which had a project within itself, led to conceptualizations which ran directly counter to the causal determinism of classical Marxist dogma.

The ability to create a break in this mechanicism (that is, the teleological objectivism of the Marxist doctrine elaborated by the Second and Third Internationals) made it possible to see the movements of capital as social movements, or as the emergence of rupture events. The revolution was not an objective end-product, an end-point to be reached by the material factors that the falling rate of profit created, but *the massive accumulation of a set of subjective processes*, an event. The thinking of Tronti and Italian *operaismo* was, in a sense, part of the 'cultural ethos' of the 1960s. In fact in France during those same years a number of writers in structuralist and then post-structuralist circles were arriving at more or less the same conclusions in their critique of deterministic causality and in their demystification of historical teleology. And this 'aura' was to be found not only in the relationship between Italy and France, and not only the environments in which

Foucauldianism or Deleuzianism formed (which were contemporaneous with the development of Italian *operaismo*): it was also to be found further afield, particularly in the US and in Latin America. We should also recall another major current which, drawing on this ethos, played its part in the transformation of Marxist historical thought: namely that of subaltern studies, which originated in India but then expanded, through post-colonial studies, into the whole English-speaking world. These writers, too, start from a historical methodology which is fundamentally Marxist, and then go on to activate it in a subjective sense.

Let us take a closer look at this group of researchers in subaltern studies. Here the historical critique starts from a radical break with the Western tradition of constructing the historical process *from above*, or rather of Eurocentric overdetermination of the history of the periphery and of the colonialized countries. Colonial historiography was a historiography which, first of all, concealed or mystified any elements that did not fit with the benevolent picture of European colonialism and, secondly, excluded people's reactions to the construction of empire – in other words, it concealed the fact that the colonial state was itself constructed as a response to struggles. The Empire is not a package of command transferred, in this instance, from Britain to India and/or elsewhere; rather, it is a series of techniques of command which we can call, Foucault-style, '*dispositifs* of power', which are recognized on the basis of a continuous and precise analysis of every moment of struggle and in relation to the modifications taking place in the relation/domination of capital. The more the capitalist system takes control of populations, the more the state and the capitalist élites feel this internalization of the working class to be ambiguous, often untenable; therefore they have to construct the state, whether colonial or not, as a response to the continuous struggles of the subjects; in short, here the autonomous initiative of subjects is placed at the centre of the analysis.

Raising the problem of causality in history – and here we begin to understand what a heavy impact causal action and the definition of its subject may have – leads us therefore to a starting question: what are these movements that we are talking about, what is this subject? The subject, or the subjectivity, of which we have spoken seems so far to have emerged by default, from a kind of splitting of the concept of capital, from the autonomization of one of its poles. Obviously we need to understand this subjectivity in terms that are more precise, more concrete. *No longer negative but constitutive.* In order to move ahead, and to specify the role of the subject when it moves within the capital relation, we therefore need to develop and deepen the definition of this process. I believe, in particular, that the solution of the two following problems can be fundamental in clarifying the methodology we are using. The first is a reading of the process in terms of a fundamental *discontinuity*. In other words, we have never considered the historical process as a linear, necessary process, defined in deterministic terms. For instance, we firmly believe that Empire exists, but it could also not exist; if it exists, this is because a series of singular forces has been brought into being, and unforeseeable events have come about. This is another way of saying that historical development in general, from the point of view of causal analysis, is not at all *prefigurable*, but always depends on the action of the subjects within the process. The action of subjects – if we relate it to the autonomy of the working class – is then always an *immeasurable* action. Immeasurable in the sense of being 'outside of measure', and also of being 'beyond measure': 'outside measure' with regard to the possibility of giving measure to, and thus controlling, these movements; 'beyond measure' in the sense that these movements can, on occasion, create situations that are completely unforeseeable, totally outside of what is thinkable.

This discussion of 'outside measure' and 'beyond measure' is the second important problem characterizing our methodology. Clearly, it connects to the advance in the critique of the classical Marxist model of historical explanation which we effected when, developing the antagonism of the capital relation, we freed it from any measure of value. In Marxism, as previously in classical economics, the concept of value constituted an internal determination, substantive to the causal explanation of historical development. When, in fact, the concept of value expresses itself as the law of value, it does so because it offers a measure to the determination of labour. The shift that we are proposing, from a closed to an open and antagonistic conception of the capital relation, *does not remove labour*, but rather *confirms its being at the centre* of every process of production and of every struggle; *it removes the measure of value* and the equilibrium of development as they had previously been determined.

The fact that we explode this determination of value does not mean that labour does not continue to be, in a fundamental sense, the basic matrix of every historical development, but only that the problem of labour (and of its liberation in the course of history) is no longer tied to those criteria of measure that characterized its birth in classical economics, from Smith through to Marx. The end of this conception means simply that we remove from the picture predeterminations that have no consistency; it means that we remove structurings of development that are purely quantitative and historically determined, but which come to be seen in universal terms. We must instead direct our research to the real transformations that lie behind the forms in which the processes of valorization present themselves. In other words, to clarify what we are saying about historical causality we have to move from a generic definition to a specific periodization of the effects of this causality. We note that the discourse on *the law of value* (typical of Marx and of classical economics) is tied to a *specific phase in the organization of labour*; a phase in which labour actually could be measured in the terms required by classical economic theory, by units of time worked. But today the process of valorization is specified in a completely different way, through the socialization of labour, and it is in these terms that historical causality needs to be defined.

We now pass to a different, albeit complementary, question: what does it mean to construct a *historical periodization*? In our case, for a start, it means to define how, within the context of capitalist development, we arrived at the end of the nation-state. Therefore it means to periodize capitalist development and to characterize specifically, within the various phases that capitalism traverses, the latest one – the imperial phase. From a methodological point of view, on the other hand, it means to assume that the capital relation is determined relative to struggles, clashes and conflicts which develop within its orbit, and that it is determined in various forms. Now, this relationship of social struggles is concretized and stabilized within Empire. If we attempt a periodization of capitalist development within modernity (or within late modernity), starting from capital's entry into the phase of *heavy industry* (which coincided with the affirmation of the nation-state), we can trace a long series of phases that lead into our present situation. Marx has already described, for his part, the entry into the age of heavy industry, showing with great lucidity how this entry was determined by the development of working-class struggles, and in particular by the shift from exploitation in terms of absolute surplus value to exploitation via the extraction of relative surplus value. It is only by superimposing the historical aspects of the Marxian narrative onto the economic analysis of the development of capital that we can grasp this periodization.

A central element, of priority in the periodization, will be the theoretical definition of 'large-scale industry' – its concept – from the point of view of the subjects, of the struggles and of the antagonistic processes of subjectivation that are active and constructed within it. In order to define the process of formation and transformation of heavy industry we can use a series of indices. I divide the period of 'heavy industry' into two broad phases. The *first phase* goes from 1870 through to the First World War, from the Paris Commune to the Russian Revolution of 1917. The *second phase* lasts from the end of the First World War to 1968. In defining these periods we have to ask what are the differences that characterize them. Or, rather, what are the differences (transformations) that characterize the proletarian subject (its technical and political composition) within the various forms of organization of labour and society. So, in the first place, *from the point of view of labour processes* and their modification; in the second place, focusing on *norms of consumption* and social reproduction; thirdly, starting from the models of *economic and political regulation*; and then, finally, examining the transformation of *political class composition*.

Let us examine the first period of 'heavy industry', the period studied particularly by Marx. From the point of view of labour processes we have a figure of a working class which is, for the first time, globally drawn under the command of machinery. The worker becomes part of the machinery, or rather its appendage. He is labour power annexed to the productive cycle. He is labour power which gradually learns new skills, being inserted into a learning process that little by little allows him a certain understanding of the work cycle. We can call this period the phase of the *skilled worker*. Compared with the period of manufacturing (which, in Marx's narrative, immediately precedes that of heavy industry), this first phase of heavy industry has a deeply transformed technical composition (in other words, the totality of the technologically efficacious capacities in working-class labour), inasmuch as here the worker is formed directly in the factory (he is no longer the artisan who is introduced, with all his difference, into manufacturing) and his status, which previously, in manufacturing, had been independent, here becomes that of a prosthesis of an increasingly massive and complex system of machinery.

Seen in terms of consumption norms, this first phase is characterized by an increasingly widespread growth of mass production, only in part subjected to an adequate capacity of social regulation on the part of capital, but which anyway is not matched by an adequate wage capacity. *Low wages* and *overproduction* are the two faces of this particular coin. This means that, in this first phase of the cycle of the skilled worker in heavy industry, the nation-state registers a productive action of capital which aims at a maximum exploitation of the workforce, and shows a less than relative ability to create equilibrium within development. It is on the wave of this crisis in mass production that we see the emergence of the search for external markets, and for imperialist and colonial outlets.

Consequently, as regards models of regulation, the state develops towards increasingly rigid levels of institutional integration with finance capital, and recognizes its political base and area of action within the development of monopolies and of imperialist consolidation. Here we are in the phase of the great analyses of *imperialism*, from Hilferding to Lenin, which dissect and render theoretically the characteristics of this period with absolute precision.

Finally, as regards the political composition of the proletariat, we have the formation of the labour movement, based on a dual form of organization (mass and vanguard; trade union and political parties) and a programme that aims at workers' control of industrial production and of the organization of society, within a programme of the socialist emancipation of the masses. It is thus in a particularly critical situation (characterized by mass production, proletarian underconsumption and imperialist expansion) that the creation and political genesis of the working-class movement come about: in this process the prevailing model is that of a reappropriation of capitalist development as such by the working class, since organization is based on the skill levels of the mass of workers and on their relative control over the cycle; and this was the basis that made possible the socialist development of the organization of society. Thus the technical composition of the worker finds a matching translation in the political composition of socialist organization and in the idea of the factory councils, which were seen as replacing the bosses after the revolution.

The values of labour and the productive capacity of factory labour were assumed to be fundamental. And, when we remember that the nation-state interprets the values of capitalist develop-ment, we will not be surprised to find that the working class identifies with the nation-state, which is the dominant trend in the parties and in the ideology of this period. The ending of the labour movement's loyalty to the nation-state only comes about during the First World War, in the dramatic way with which we are familiar, and is realized and represented in the Bolshevik Revolution and in the cycle of struggles that carried through into the 1920s.

The second phase of 'heavy industry' lasted until 1968. Study-ing this phase will allow us to define, or at least to begin the analysis of, the situation in which we find ourselves today – a highly dramatic situation, in which the relationship between the technical composition of labour and the political composition of the working class (later we shall speak of this as 'the multitude') is open to completely new alternatives.

Now, considering this period that runs up to 1968, taking this symbolic date as an indicator of a point of arrival and of a further modification in modes of working, we shall try to analyse the second phase of the cycle of heavy industry under its threefold aspects of labour processes, norms of consumption and regula-tion, which will enable us to identify the new technical and political composition of the proletariat during that second phase.

As regards labour processes, the new technical composition of the proletariat becomes an 'abstract' labour power, in the sense that it is abstracted from any concrete quality and is annexed as such to the industrial process, in the forms of *Taylorism*. Taylorist norms make it possible to insert large masses of unskilled and de-skilled workers into labour processes that are very complex and alienating. Here the *mass worker* completely loses sight of the overall productive cycle.

As regards consumption norms, this is the phase in which *Fordism* is constituted, in other words a capitalist practice in which the wage is seen as an advance geared to the purchase and consumption of the commodities created by mass-production industry. Consumerist alienation is a first consequence of this model of regulation. But more than that: the relationship that the consumption norms determine has immediate consequences for the overall cycle, in the sense that it imposes an effective inner regulation. It is no accident that the *regulation model* that is asserted is the *Keynesian* one, in other words, a model that tries to fix and maintain, in a continuous way, an equilibrium between productive capacities and effective demand on the part of the workers.

As regards regulation norms, we see the gradual formation, solicited by Keynesian policies, of a model of the *interventionist state* which supports productive activity, maintains full employment and provides social welfare (spending of the deferred wage). Here the relation, within capitalist development, between capital and the working class was altered to the advantage of the working class, bringing about situations in which equilibrium was given by a variety of institutional figures (the democratic New Deal state, the corporatist and fascist state, the socialist state and so on).

As regards the political composition of the proletariat, we have an extension of the experiences of the socialist working-class organizations. There was the emergence, especially in the US and in the more advanced capitalist countries, of new forms of organization. In these forms of organization of the mass worker, the main slogans were: the *refusal of work*, trade-union egalitarianism, rejection of any figure of delegation and the reappropriation of power, in rank and file and mass forms. This was something of the experience that we had in Italy during the 1960s and 1970s, and which we were also able to observe at the international level.

However, before continuing with this periodization, we need to ask ourselves how the relation between forms of class composition and capital is determined. How and why do we establish this relation? Why, in speaking about forms of life, of organization of working-class reproduction, do we also talk about the state? On this point a number of clarifications need to be made. As is well-known, in Marx's *Capital* there is no book on the state. In *Empire* we maintain that this lack is linked substantially to the lack of an analysis of the organization of the world market – another argument not dealt with in *Capital*. Now we know that the state, as it imposes itself within capitalist development, is a regulatory force. But its capacity for regulation is based on, and consolidated by, relations that are still external to capitalist development itself. In this sense Marx has a problem when speaking of the state of capital, inasmuch as he has to locate it within a schema of control of the world market: Marx does not succeed in conceiving it as the national state (of capital). What Marx needs is a general schema of capitalist development, and this general schema can be only given at the global level. *In fact, Marx considers the nation-state as an obstacle to capitalist development* and a leftover of the pre-capitalist era, where (quite to the contrary) it had been a formidable lever for primitive accumulation.

Now let us return to the analysis of *the shift that takes place in the 1970s* and which allows us, in terms of periodization, to see its further determination. The new phase is characterized by various radical elements of innovation. The first innovation has to do with changes taking place in the labour processes: these involve processes of automation in the factories and of informatization of society, in other words the setting to work of the whole of society. Directly productive material labour loses its centrality in the production process, and what emerges is the new figure of the *socialized worker*, which presents itself as the interpreter of the functions of labour cooperation manifested within the social productive networks. These new figures of labour power, cooperating at the social level, become central and hegemonic in the production process.

As for consumption norms, they are generally related to market choices, and from this point of view they express themselves as widespread forms of *individualism*, which follows on the social diffusion and singularization of production.

As regards regulation models, as a result of the developments described above they extend along *multinational lines*, passing in a first phase through monetary dimensions, then through the financial market and, finally, through the concretization of the political–imperial function.

As for the composition of the proletariat, it becomes social, but it is increasingly *immaterial* as regards the substance of its labour. In form, it is also mobile, multiform and flexible.

I want to stress one final point, again at the level of method. If the things that I have said work, and if in some way there begins to emerge a schema of causal relation as regards the the genesis of Empire and the inner order of *Empire*, we find ourselves here in a critical situation in which the categories of labour, the concept of capital, the concept of the state, the definitions of right and of nation, the categories of international law and therefore of international society and so on, which modernity has left us, are probably obsolete. However, if we have to begin to operate with other conceptual determinations, this means that we are facing a quali-tative leap, in which the motive forces and the processes that up to now have supported our reasoning on the causations and transformation of capital's various eras are themselves in some sense brought into question. In other words, the fact that such an event as the constitution of a global command exists means that there is a leap in the scientific explanation, which modifies everything, obliging us to reconsider the categories we have worked with up until now and to consider previous categories as destined for obsolescence.

We speak of *a transition from modernity to postmodernity* as a way of summing up all the various 'post-' categories (post-Taylorist, post-Fordist, post-Keynesian, post-socialist, post-communist and so on). It is obvious that when we use the term 'postmodern', we use it rather differently from the way it was used by the philosophers of the last quarter of the twentieth century. In particular, it is obvious that we speak of it in terms of a *grand narrative*, which is exactly what was forbidden by Lyotard, Baudrillard and in general by all those who initially used the term postmodern to formulate a way of considering the historical present.

Note, by the way, that there is a simliar position constructed in legal and sociological studies, which is expressed for instance by German writers such as Ulrich Beck, but also by French writers. They reject the term 'postmodern', preferring instead to use 'hypermodernity' or 'late modernity'. In reality, what lies behind this nominalistic disagreement is a refusal by these writers to accept that the categories of modernity have come to an end. When they oppose the use of the term 'postmodern' they do so because they think that, despite everything, there is still a possibility of preserving and using words and concepts such as nation-state, international law, and the like. We, for our part, insist on a conception of historical causation which finds in the dynamics of struggles the reason for changes in historical realities, for conceptual rupture, and therefore for the necessity of establishing a new vocabulary.

Earlier I said that Marx saw the nation-state as an obstacle to capitalist development, as a remnant of the pre-capitalist age which, although it had been a formidable lever for primitive accumulation, nevertheless remained something only partially identifiable with capital. However Marx's position here needs to be analysed in relation to the political development of the capitalist forms of accumulation. And, while undoubtedly the distinction between sovereignty and capital (between the concept of sovereignty and that of capital) is deep precisely in the first phase, gradually, as capitalist development gets under way, relations are formed between the two concepts, if not of homology or identity, then certainly of analogy. To the extent that society comes to be subsumed within capital (passing from the *formal subsumption of labour* to *real subsumption*), every social relationship becomes in some sense a productive relationship: and at that moment *the relations of sovereignty and of capital become in some way superimposable*. Real subsumption involves the capitalization of the social: consequently, the centre of gravity of exploitation shifts directly to the social. The crisis of the law of value, and therefore the non-measurability of the relationship of exploitation and expropriation which by now operates at every social nexus – and in particular over cooperation – leads to an immediacy of command. Therefore here, in real subsumption, command is no longer something added from outside of the exploitation process, but something which organizes it directly. In saying this we recognize a kind of liminal identity, or at least a kind of deep homology, between the concept of sovereignty and the concept of capital.

All this applies not only to the evolution of the nation-state; it applies particularly transversally to the definition of global *governance*. Global governance is directly inherent to the capitalist logic of development. And here there is no longer space for a theory of sovereignty of the kind constructed in nihilist terms by Carl Schmitt. The decision over the space of exception is refined to the point where it becomes a function of capitalist necessity. The obedience of the subjected will no longer be formed on a unilateral base but will interpret the capitalist relation.

(However, on all this, see the notes on the concept of sovereignty which follow this lesson.)

So, in dealing with historical method we have tried to reformulate a theory of historical causality drawing, on the one hand, on the Historical Writings *of Karl Marx and, on the other, on the re-elaboration of Marx by Mario Tronti in his* Operai e capitale *(Einaudi, Turin 1966). Another very important area for us has been that of the subaltern studies of the Indian school of Ranajit Guha (see* Selected Subaltern Studies, *ed. R. Guha and G. C. Spivak, Oxford University Press, Oxford, 1988). However, the issue which has to be addressed here is that of* the teleological function that causal determination expresses. *Critics of Marxism (and also of* operaismo*) attack Marxian causality (even where it is represented by processes of struggle) as a deterministic relation. I do not believe that this critique is valid, even though there is no doubt that in historical materialism dialectical instances survive which are often heavy with deterministic tendencies. Moreover, the economistic determinations of some parts of the* Capital *do not help in getting round this difficulty.*

I believe that within operaismo *the problem has been faced, broadly and effectively, so that today the type of methodology proposed incorporates a series of elements which radically modify its definition and exclude surreptitious determinist interpretations. Already in my* Macchina tempo *(published in* Time for Revolution, *Continuum International, London, 2003) the continuity and discontinuity of Marxian time, in other words, of the time of struggles, are considered within a horizon that is absolutely* untimely. *In particular, in rendering itself discontinuous, capitalist temporality becomes* constitutive, *the untimeliness opens to subjectivity. Plainly we have here deep analogies with the earlier discussion of real subsumption and the socialization of nexuses of accumulation in becoming social, these nexuses are, so to speak, subjectivated. An ontological transition thus comes about in the discontinuity of productive time, and constituted being is always and anew a constituent being.*

As regards the issues of historical causality, once again, see my Marx beyond Marx *(Autonomedia, New York, 1992). In this case, in attempting to free Marxian thought from determinist ties, the analysis of cause shifts away from the (more or less dialectical) mechanicist horizon to the theory of the dispositif. In this case too, bearing in mind the*

Foucauldian and Deleuzian origins of the theory of the dispositif, *we have a displacement from the objective to the subjective, to a definition of cause as being structured by constitutive acts. We are within onto-logical causation. The demystification of the capitalist relationship carried out by Tronti, turning it into an* intersubjective relationship *(capital as a relationship, with workers and capital in opposition to each other), now develops so as to take a* constitutive dimension. *I believe that in this way the rearticulation of a theory of historical causation has become plausible.*

Naturally, as regards problems of periodization, we must bear in mind the same presuppositions. Of the two tracks that we have followed, one is tied to the transformation taking place in the categories of work, and we could define it as from primitive accumulation to the he-gemony of the immaterial; *the other assumes the relationship between categories of labour and categories of the state, and it could therefore be defined as* the imperial overcoming of the nation-state. *At the root of both these points of view stands the understanding of the transition from modernity to postmodernity. That this transition can be narrated, I have shown (together with Michael Hardt) in* Labor of Dionysus: A Critique of the State Form, *University of Minnesota Press, Minnesota, 2005. As for relations between the category of labour and the category of the state, see the formidable contribution of Luciano Ferrari Bravo,* Dal Fordismo alla globalizazzione [From Fordism to Globalization] *(Manifestolibri, Rome 2001). A more extended treatment of the question of periodization can be seen in my twenty theses published as 'Interpretation of the class situation today: Method-ological aspects', in* Open Marxism, *vol. II, Pluto Press, London, 1992, pp. 69–105. Naturally, having perfected the analytical path, we arrive at the definition of a new paradigm: to be specific, that of the hegemony of immaterial labour, i.e. the model of general intellect. For a discus-sion of all this see Lesson 2.*

4

Sovereignty*

Michael Hardt and Antonio Negri

Limited sovereignty and 11 September

The attacks on New York and Washington on 11 September 2001 did not change the condition of sovereignty, but they did perhaps reveal more clearly a change that had already taken place. In particular, they revealed the inadequacy of any substantialist notion of sovereignty: sovereignty is not an autonomous substance but rather a relationship between the ruler and the ruled. Sovereign power is never absolute. It constantly seeks to establish and reproduce its hegemony over the ruled. The one who obeys is thus no less essential to the conception and functioning of sovereignty than the one who commands. Consequently, there is no exclusive source of sovereignty as the substantialist notion would have it.

One might say that 11 September showed definitively that the US is part of the world or, really, that the US government is not an autonomous source of sovereignty but rather part of a global series of relationships that define the present form of sovereignty.

Throughout the modern era, the international scene was composed by a set of dominant sovereign national powers which posed

* Text presented to the American Association of Anthropology, Washington, December 2001.

external limits on each other's sovereignty and ruled over the subordinated nations and regions. In our current transition towards Empire, however, the sovereignty of the dominant nation-states is being compromised, while sovereignty is being transferred to, and transformed by, a new imperial power, which is supranational and tends towards global control. In one sense, then, one might say that this imperial sovereignty is unlimited externally insofar as, in a certain sense, it envelops the entire globe. Imperial sovereignty has no outside. In another sense, however, sovereignty remains (and must always remain) limited internally by the relationship between the ruler and the ruled. Sovereignty is in this sense always double-faced; it is, necessarily, a dual system of power.

Since in the transition to Empire the external limits of sovereignty tend to disappear, the concept of war, understood as the conflict between sovereign powers, has little significance. Social conflicts of sovereignty tend instead to accumulate on the internal boundaries. These internal lines of division are what always and inevitably determine, within sovereignty, the possibility of civil war. In Empire, civil war – along with the police action that works constantly to prevent its eruption – is the only adequate expression of the double-faced nature of sovereignty. The events of 11 September were not the beginning of this imperial civil war. We have now been for some time in something like a permanent state of civil war, even in what was thought to be peacetime. We have to understand the complex and multiple lines of this civil war that defines imperial sovereignty and discover how it can be transformed into a liberatory struggle which could lead to a genuine peace.

Molar and molecular histories

First, we need to step back and look more closely at this new form of sovereignty in its period of formation. In the framework of the analysis of political regimes, one can see that sovereignty has been transformed from the form typical of modern European imperialisms, into the contemporary form of Empire. The Cold War was the principal period of this transition. The transformation of sovereignty during the period of the Cold War, however, appears very different depending on whether one adopts a molar or a molecular perspective on the workings of sovereignty. We should explain, very briefly, that the difference between the molar and the molecular does not refer merely to size, nor does it refer to the difference between the individual and the collective. Molecular and molar both indicate social collectivities; the terms refer to two kinds of collections or populations. The molar refers to large aggregates or statistical groupings that form a bounded and unified whole through a process of integration and representation. The molecular refers, on the other hand, to micromultiplicities or rather singularities, which form unbounded constellations or networks.

From the molar perspective, then, the form or nature of sovereignty does not really change during the period of the Cold War. The transition appears rather as the progressive reduction of the number of sovereign powers, from several to two, then to one. Prior to the Cold War, during the age of European imperialism, there were several sovereign powers, primarily the European nation-states, in constant competition. The form of sovereignty involved in the imperialist projects was defined by the sovereignty of the nation-states. Imperialism was simply the extension of national sovereignty over foreign territory. From this molar perspective, the Cold War represented a continuity of the imperialist form of sovereignty: the two great power blocs, or the two superpowers, had merely taken over from the European nation-states and consolidated the competition along a single line. In the Second World, the Soviets demonstrated repeatedly that the different nations of Eastern Europe were not sovereign, but Soviet hegemony was never complete. (Most notably, China and Yugoslavia successfully obtained considerable margins of autonomy.) Similarly, in the First World different nation-states maintained relative degrees of independence, particularly in Western Europe, but finally they, too, could not resist the bi-polar forces of the superpower divide. The different nation-states in the Third World, whether or not newly formed after liberation from colonial rule, were clearly not sovereign; they were forced to line up behind one superpower or the other. In the last instance, nuclear arsenals determined sovereignty for the bi-polar world. In short, from this molar perspective, the period of the Cold War involved the tendency (which was never complete and absolute) to undermine all sovereignties except those of the two superpowers.

It is logical to assume from this perspective that the post-Cold War world must be defined by a single superpower, the only remaining sovereign power. This is a history of purely quantitative differences: as the number of sovereign powers diminishes, the scale of sovereignty increases, but there is no change in the form of sovereignty itself.

From the molecular perspective, however, we can see that during the period of the Cold War there was a transformation of the very form of sovereignty. The Cold War appears not as the global extension of the conflict between sovereign national powers but rather as the erosion of national sovereignty itself and, consequently, as the formation of a new, non-national sovereignty.

The shift in the form of sovereignty can be best recognized by the emergent conceptions of the enemy within the United States during the Cold War. In effect, the United States had to confront two types of communist enemy: whereas from the molar perspective the communist enemy could be located in another sovereign power – the Soviet Union – from the molecular perspective the communist enemy was nebulous, fleeting and spectral. The molecular communist enemy was potentially every-where, throughout the US and indeed throughout the world. The enemy was ungraspable and continually disappeared in the crowd, just as it disappeared in the jungle. The enemy was not, in other words, a stable sovereign subject, but an elusive and amorphous network that could not be contained within bound-aries – a con-tagious virus, perhaps, rather than a bounded, autonomous entity.

McCarthyism was one manifestation of the hysteria that results when a sovereign power confronts such an unlocalizable and ubiquitous threat. The battle against a non-sovereign enemy – an enemy both inside and outside – tends to erode the sovereignty of the nation-state itself. One of the fundamental conditions of sovereignty, the ability to exclude external sources of authority from the domestic territory, becomes virtually impossible, as there is progressively less distinction between inside and outside. (This pervasive, invisible enemy is perhaps a symptom rather than a cause of the transformation of national sovereignty.)

The result of this molecular history is the appearance of a new form of sovereignty, which has no outside or, rather, recognizes no difference between inside and outside. From this perspective, the Cold War is a period of historical shift rather than continuity: with the decline of the national form of sovereignty arises a new, global form.

These two perspectives, of course, have not always been given equal value. During the Cold War, the molecular level was continually overcoded by the molar. In the US, for example, there was a tendency to project not only all communist and socialist activity, along with the corresponding labour organizations, but indeed all social difference and contestation, onto the bi-polar divide. Any social threat or refusal could be cast as un-American, and thus as being in league with the sovereign enemy. In perfectly specular fashion, the Soviets, too, projected all forms of internal threats onto the external enemy. This overcoding was even more pronounced in the context of Third World liberation struggles, which had to code themselves, on pain of death, with one or the other sovereign power. In each case, the molecular specificity and multiplicity of the different social expressions were masked by the molar frame.

Today, however, it is clear that the molecular developments were really the primary and effective ones – and in retrospect we can see that perhaps the molecular forces have always been primary. Today's world is one in which no nation-state, not even the most powerful, is sovereign. And the enemies that appear are not nation-states either. The enemies are instead pervasive, un-localizable, and invisible networks. Today the image of a sovereign enemy nation-state and the kind of war it allows is merely an illusion, based perhaps on a nostalgia for a by-gone world.

Contradictions of sovereignty

Sovereignty is thus defined by a molecular dynamics which constantly puts pressure on its internal limit, and thus highlights its double-faced nature. Once we recognize sovereignty as a double-faced concept, as a hegemonic relationship, we can recognize a series of contradictions which plagued sovereignty throughout the modern era and extend into our imperial age. Consider first of all the modern military figure of sovereignty, that is, the power to decide on the life and death of subjects. Nuclear weapons, from one perspective, made this prerogative of sovereignty absolute.

This absolute power, however, is radically thrown into question by practices such as suicidal actions, from the protest of the Buddhist monk who sets himself on fire in Vietnam to the terrorist suicide bomber. When life itself is negated in the struggle to challenge imperial sovereignty, the power over life and death that the sovereign exercises becomes useless. The absolute weapons aimed against bodies are neutralized by the voluntary and absolute negation of the body. In other words, sovereign warfare, which in the age of Empire becomes a technology of control that mixes military and police action, loses its stable foundation when confronted with biopolitical forms of contestation. Sovereignty, in this case, not only cannot pretend to be absolute, but is thrown decisively into crisis. In this context sovereignty must necessarily be dialogical.

There is a similar development in the world of business and finance. The power to mint money and control currencies defines economic sovereignty, but this too has undergone an imperial transformation. There are, of course, a few dominant currencies (the dollar, the euro, the pound and the yen) which are controlled to a certain extent by state structures, but there has also developed an enormous process of private regulation of capitalist relationships. The *lex mercatoria* [merchant law] was the unified customary trade law of medieval merchants, an international commercial law that functioned outside of either public law or common law, regulating trade relationships – for example, at the great medieval fairs. Today a postmodern *lex mercatoria* is forming, a transnational customary law founded on the shared legal understandings of an international community composed principally of commercial, shipping, insurance, and banking enterprises. Many aspects of global business relations are regulated by this well-developed and articulated legal sphere, defined by contracts and financial mechanisms where, for the most part, it is the law firms that make the law. This transnational commercial law functions, to a large degree, independently of the legal frameworks of the nation-states. But who guarantees the *lex mercatoria* in this situation? Especially in cases where conflict threatens imperial authority? In such cases the *lex mercatoria* cannot cover the risk and insure present and future economic values. In this strange conjuncture, the concept of sovereignty opens up once again and shows its double-faced nature. The sovereign power is called upon to guarantee and insure the *lex mercatoria* but such insurance is always a relationship of inclusion based proportionally on the needs of all parties. What results is a strange, almost democratic, mercantile relationship, a form of dialogue.

A third example, after the crisis of war technology and the crisis of insurance and risk, has to do with power and the need to control languages. Today, in post-Fordist production, language itself has become a productive force. The entire set of signs has been entrusted to the creativity of living labour: this is what constitutes the dominant form of creativity in our society. One works with languages and constructs with signs. At this point, control over the meanings and references of signs, languages and productive systems is something that exceeds any possible linear relationship, and hence any absolute or unilateral control. In this case too, just as in the case of the suicide attack that undermines sovereign violence, the creative field of meaning erodes the possibility of absolute control over languages.

If these are some of the conditions of sovereignty in Empire, then every aspect of absolute sovereign control is thrown off balance. Military power must, sooner or later, ask its adversaries to join the game. The *lex mercatoria* must sooner or later ask its insurers to bring the state (and the multitude) into the game. And, today more than ever before, no form of domination or dictatorship can both control languages and promote linguistic production, since languages are not simply instruments of communication but are themselves immediately productive. In each of these respects, Empire is constrained to recognize its internal limits and its double-faced nature.

Civil war

If we have now entered a world in which there is only one sovereign power, not a nation-state but a global form of sovereignty that has no outside, then every war is necessarily a civil war, in the sense that it is a conflict within a single society, now a global society. Competing molar and molecular perspectives reappear here as different interpretations of civil war. According to the molar perspective, a civil war is characterized by the conflict between two potentially separate and sovereign powers. This perspective would see, for example, the nineteenth-century civil war in the US as the unionist North against the secessionist South. In our own time, Samuel Huntington's clash-of-civilizations theory proposes such a molar perspective: potentially sovereign and territorially separate civilizational blocs struggle with each other for autonomy and hegemony within the global system. A molecular perspective, however, reveals a very different image of civil war. Molecular civil war is defined by overlapping networks that conflict, in one common space, along a multiplicity of modulating fronts. Once again, this molecular perspective is closer to reality.

At the beginnings of European modernity, sovereignty was posed in two different modalities. The first modality was monarchy, that is, the claim to unity of power and to its absence of internal limits. Today this modality of sovereignty is no longer possible. Sovereign cannot today, even with extreme efforts, arrive at unity; instead, its double-faced nature reappears continually. The instability of sovereign power in Empire is thus part of its definition. The insecurity of postmodernity refers not so much to society but to sovereign power. The second modality of the constitution of modern European sovereign power consisted in the construction of a people who could serve as an interlocutor of the sovereign. Today, this construction too is no longer possible. There are no more peoples but only the multitudes who follow molecular dynamics, affirm differences, and experiment in hybridization and miscegenation.

These are the conditions in which the concept of imperial sovereignty opens up to the concept of civil war. This is not a molar civil war – sovereign power will be frustrated every time it tries to name its enemy as the unified source of Evil – but a molecular, dissipative civil war. In the very moment when Empire is formed, imperial sovereignty is thrown into crisis not because it is threatened by an external enemy (there is no more outside of Empire) but by a multitude of internal, omnilateral and diffuse tensions. Sovereignty is thus here a relative, not an absolute, power that functions on the hypothesis that it can resolve the multiple tensions and from time to time intervene in the spatio-temporal decomposition of the relations of force. As Heraclitus said, sovereignty is war and war is never defined simply by two but by a multiplicity, a multitude. There is no guarantee that the civil wars that emerge in Empire will present any liberatory possibilities. In fact, the vast majority that are carried out in the name of the poor, or the oppressed, or the virtuous, are merely struggles for superiority within the hierarchies of imperial power. Today, forces which claim to represent the interests of the wretched of the earth clash with others, which pretend to represent justice and peace for all, but such civil wars are nothing but complex power struggles within the hierarchies of imperial power. How can we discover a different axis of civil war that would oppose the multitude against imperial control itself? How can we conceive and realize, not only a shift in the hierarchies of imperial power, but an overthrow of sovereignty as such, and the construction of a global democracy without sovereignty? How can a civil war that runs throughout imperial society come to an end and arrive at a genuine peace? We are certainly not yet in the position to give adequate responses to these questions, but they represent today the central problem of any possible theory of imperial sovereignty. Such a theory would have to address the molecular pressures of the multitude on the substantial ambiguity – the two-sided nature – of sovereign power.

Some archaeological traditions

The European political cultures of the nineteenth and twentieth centuries tried to reduce the concept of sovereignty to an absolute apparatus that would function without internal limits. Carl Schmitt is the author who was best able to formulate this concept, renewing the early modern theories of absolute sovereignty articulated by authors such as Jean Bodin and Thomas Hobbes. *Vitae necisque potestas* (power over life and death) is, in this context, the ultimate unilateral definition of sovereign power. Giorgio Agamben, in similar fashion, has sought to identify the ancient form of the ban as the essence of the sovereign state of exception. All of this no longer works. The end of the twentieth century brought us a realist theory of sovereignty, which shows the latter to be the result of the battle among multiple powers. Machiavelli and republicanism thus triumph over Bodin and Schmitt.

The crisis of sovereignty today is serious and profound. The king really has no clothes. Sovereignty tends to become simply useless domination. In fact, as we have seen, it is not enough to have a monopoly of military power, monetary power, and linguistic power to rule. The prospect of transforming sovereignty into an absolute power is an illusion. And it can end in tragic delirium. Along with the postmodern collapse of the parameters of national sovereignty and with the constitution and development of imperial processes, we are witnessing, and will continue to witness, attempts by the dominant powers to occupy, unilaterally, the centre of Empire, that is, the non-place of imperial power, reconstructing the concept of sovereignty as a power without internal limits.

The materialist interpretation of history is one avenue that has allowed us to recognize that the functioning of sovereignty has always been antagonistic. The analysis of the modes of production, for example, insofar as they constantly imply the active participation of the multitude in productive activity, demonstrates the transformations of the forms of rule and their effectiveness. From the point of view of the analysis of different regimes of production, the *homo sacer* that Agamben evokes is more of a slave in flight than a figure of the mythic archaeology of law; he is the German peasant in the sixteenth-century land wars, already exploited and rebellious; he is the nineteenth-century proletarian who tries to reappropriate the products of labour through violent struggles. In short, all this demonstrates that sovereignty functions fundamentally by dominating the poor and exploiting its expressive capacity. But, since this expressive capacity is production itself, the poor must continue to express itself if life is to continue. Any absolute notion of sovereignty is thrown off balance by these contradictions. Sovereignty in the imperial conditions is an omnilateral antagonism that must confront the subjects who produce. This antagonism is what defines the forms and the actors of a dialogue, not a contradiction that can be superseded and subsumed.

Sovereignty and war

There are some who think that it is possible to control or contain the multilateral forces of globalization by restoring the old world of the nation-state and its modern sovereignty. In France, some of them are called '*souverainistes*' and, in the US, others (with a very different ideological agenda) go under the name of unilateralists, but more or less everywhere one can find this conservative tendency. Even at Porto Alegre, in the happy public spaces of the intercontinental march of liberation, one can find such affirmations. It is easy to respond that globalization cannot be turned back, at whatever costs, and that, in particular, it is impossible to reconstruct the old form of sovereignty. This said, however, it is worth adding that globalization can be desirable and can correspond to, and be part of, a revolutionary process: in the modern era, this involved the revolt of the working classes in the dominant regions of the globe and their desire to negate themselves as a class, along with the liberation struggles of colonial peoples and with their desire to negate themselves as peoples. Within globalization, the very possibility of sovereignty can be destroyed by such a regime of desire. This desire is brought to the fore by the civil war that tears apart imperial domination. Whoever wants to travel the path of the liberation of the multitudes must take account of this terrific possibility, offered by the transformations of sovereignty into imperial civil war. This is a project worthy of the multitude: transform the oppressive state of permanent war in which we find ourselves into a liberatory war which can eventually lead to an authentic social peace.

5

LESSON 2

On Social Ontology: Material Labour, Immaterial Labour and Biopolitics

I would like to continue from what has been said thus far by looking at the question of methodology in terms of historical sequences. The conclusion is clear: when a new configuration of the historical fabric comes into being, we have at the same time a shift in epistemological perspective. Methods of knowledge and of a real approach to facts will be modified, particularly *in practical terms*, in other words, in terms of an insertion of episteme into reality, which means from the point of view of mechanisms of action. Thus, *every time the historical context changes, method changes as well*. There is no such thing as a method which is universal and 'for ever'. Or rather: there are specifically determined universal methods, methods which are valid 'generally' in given situations and at given times. The determination of method is as important as its universality. This is the problem that we face today when we address, for example, Marx's famous *Einleitung*, the introduction to his *Grundrisse* of 1857. In our younger days we were persecuted by a Marxist orthodoxy which imposed those methodological determinations on us as necessities. But things could not carry on like that. The positive construction enacted by Marx's method corresponded to a situation which was real and singular, characterized by the relations of production of the mid-nineteenth century. We, however, in specifying our own methodology, are obliged to develop our analysis on the basis of the real world as it exists in our own century and on our own social stage. It is in relation to all this that we shall seek to elaborate a method which is matched to, and effective within, this situation.

I would start by saying that we are in an extremely difficult theoretical situation, because we must, at one and the same time, define the method and determine the thing itself, that is, the situation which is to be analysed. Now, the object that method has to approach in our present and actual situation is difficult to grasp – probably because a very important structural change has taken place. Let us bear in mind that, in the past, methodological thinking had always assumed *a certain duality* between the point of observation and the object observed. But today it appears that there no longer exists *an outside*. This is precisely one of the methodological issues on which we base our discussion of Empire. If there is no more an outside, this involves a certain difficulty in dealing with the matter, or the object, that we are hoping to define. We are inside, not outside; we move within. This fact of 'being immersed' explodes the generally available methodological criteria, which were based on being able to address themselves, from the outside, to something that was stable and thereby able to elicit the narrative from that objective stability which determines historical relations, fixes them and gives them meaning. Furthermore: what normally follows from this awareness – namely that of being immersed – is a strongly relativistic way of seeing things. And what normally follows cognitive relativism is ethical scepticism. But we, moving in the spirit of Marx, would say that this relativistic method expresses a position that is absolute. We say that cognitive relativism can *take a position* within the real that it traverses, and that it can reconstruct it, placing itself on the inside as a common ethical consciousness: we speak in terms of a common ethics of responsibility.

In Marx's *Einleitung*[*Introduction*] there was, in effect, still an outside which was within the method and which absolutized it, and this 'outside' was the concept of *use value*. It determined the fixity on the basis of which method could consolidate itself, before embarking on the adventure of the ever-new discovery of the real. As is well known, Marx said that everything was produced between nature and culture. In the process of history everything had either a use value or an exchange value. *Use value* was something that was, so to speak, *in the nature of* the commodity object; exchange value, on the other hand, derived from the socio-political relationships within the overall development of the means of production. An extreme example: labour power itself was initially a pure use value before it became a commodity, in other words an exchange value on the market.

Today we are in a situation where the use value is completely transformed and remodelled (this is the first thing to be noted, as regards the ontology of social being). In Lesson 1 we said: we are awaiting a radical innovation, an event, even *a monster*. In reality, the monster is already with us: namely the transformations in the form of labour, in the force of production: the dematerialized form in which we act in order to produce goods and in order to construct the world. Furthermore, with ever-greater conviction, we learn that it is our capacity for knowledge that allows us today to access production and, through it, inter-human relations and the reproduction of social being. This is why we need to develop an *ontology of immaterial labour*, or rather an *ontology of immaterial being* which has within it a hegemony of immaterial labour – where by 'immaterial labour' we mean the ensemble of intellectual, communicative, relational and affective activities which are expressed by subjects and social movements – for them to lead to production.

The foundations of this hypothesis, which is both methodological and substantive, go back to Marx's text, known as the 'Fragment on machinery'. In this fundamental section of the *Grundrisse*, Marx develops a hypothesis on the development of the labour form in the future development of capitalism. His hypothesis is that labour will become increasingly immaterial. In other words, it will depend fundamentally on the intellectual and scientific energies that constitute it. Marx says that labour which has reached that immaterial quality and is organized by intellectual and scientific energies renders unnecessary and ineffective (in other words destroys) the conditions within which accumulation has developed up to that point.

Consequently, it renders irrelevant the measurement of labour time as a norm for fixing an order of labour in the world: but of that we have already spoken extensively. The working day, Marx tells us, is no longer reducible to labour time pure and simple.

Sometimes – he adds – the time of labour becomes a minor concern, when one considers the totality of production (no longer simply of factories but) of capitalist society a whole. Whereas previously, in order to produce a commodity, what was required was a certain number of hours of simple labour (another naturalistic illusion), or at any rate, in order to produce a greater number of goods an increase in the mass of labour was necessary, what we find today is that every increase of production comes as an expression of intellectual activities from the productive force of scientific invention, and above all from the close application of science and technology in elaborating the activity of transformation of matter. Hence we are faced with a radical modification in the function of productive time (and also of historical time). It will be obvious, for example, that the time of education and training becomes far more important than the time of immediate application to production; the time of external relations that nourish consciousness and push it towards actions and mental decisions will become more important than the accumulation of small temporal amounts of labour which are no longer – as they once were – the precondition for lift-off of the capitalist realization of value.

We are thus in a situation where *labour time* on the one hand and, on the other, the *criterion of measure* of this time (and hence the law of value) become less and less important as *central quantifying elements of production*. It will be, rather, the social and collective individual who will determine the value of production, since, given that labour is organized in communicative and linguistic forms, and given that knowledge is something cooperative, production will depend increasingly on the unity of connections and relations that constitute intellectual and linguistic labour, in other words it will be dependent on this *collective individual*.

At this point in Marx two lines emerge. The first line is the prediction that labour will become the labour of overseeing machines. We will thus have plenty of free time; and it is no accident that it is in these pages that we find the praise of Fourier, the exaltation of joy and free time. Then there is a second line, far more realistic than the former, which examines the coincidence between life time and labour time.

This latter is not a Marxian utopia. Or rather, what might once have looked like utopia has now become reality. Today we find ourselves in a way of life and in a way of producing that are characterized by the hegemony of intellectual labour. It has been said that we have entered the era of *cognitive capitalism*. People are studying the forms in which capitalism expresses itself and determines its development through these changes. People even talk about a *third capitalist transition*, after the phase of manufacturing and the subsequent phase of heavy industry. In this cognitive era the production of value depends increasingly on creative intellectual activity which, apart from placing itself beyond any valorization related to scarcity, also places itself beyond mass accumulation, factory accumulation and the like. *The originality of cognitive capitalism consists in capturing, within a generalized social activity, the innovative elements which produce value.*

What in Schumpeter was considered a marginal element in defining innovative development, or in fact the appreciation of that new element which, breaking productive repetition, created value and generated development, today becomes a feature that characterizes the whole of development. So here we are defining something completely internal to that context which earlier we took as our starting point, when we said that there is no longer an 'outside', not even a marginal outside. Hence, *capitalist development and the capitalist creation of value are based more and more on the concept of social capture of value itself.* The capture of this innovation, an expression of creative activity, is the result of a growing socialization of production. This in turn means: the enterprise must have the ability to valorize the wealth produced by networks that do not belong to it; the enterprise (and thus also the organization of cognitive capitalism) is increasingly based on a capacity for private appropriation, imposed through the capture of the social flows of cognitive labour. It follows from this that exploitation goes back to being, once again, the extraction of absolute surplus value, since, in order to produce, capital employs only command.

When we address the theme of command as being central in the extraction of surplus value and fundamental in defining exploitation, we can begin to refer to the capitalist function as parasitic. However, we should be careful not to mystify this perception. The progressive function of capital, as Marx described it in *Capital* and as it was then taken up by the communist tradition, has also played a fundamental role for us too, insofar as we have seen globalization constituting itself as a production of struggles, but also as effective modernization imposed by capital. However, today we are faced with a crisis of this progressive function. Crisis or end, *crisis* or *catastrophe*? We can say that the great crisis derives from the fact that we are witnessing the so-called 'end of the dialectics of the instrument', where by instrumentality we mean the fact that capital provided the worker with the instrument of labour. When the human brain reappropriates the instrument of labour, capital no longer has the possibility of articulating command over the instrument: and thus the instrumental dialectics exhausts itself. Let us set this problem from another point of view, namely by looking at capitalist development from the point of view of techniques of political control. For as long as the instrumental dialectics still exists, capital will discipline individuals and will control populations within production and within reproduction. But when the entire paradigmatic framework of labour is changed, when labour comes to consist of a totality of knowledge borne and put into production by mass intellectuality, then political control comes to be exercised through war. War (and only war) is thus the form of control exercised by parasitic capital; war is the crisis that becomes the *dispositif* of capitalist order.

Let us look at this business of *parasitic capital* from another point of view, this time *in terms of the socialization of labour*. Here capital becomes productive only to the extent that it captures values preconstituted by social labour. So here the command function is organized as a threat to block information, as an interruption of the cognitive processes. In short, we can say that parasitic capital is that capital which draws value from the *arresting* of the movements of knowledge, cooperation and language. In order to live and reproduce himself, the capitalist is forced to blackmail society and to block the social processes of production every time they present themselves as excedent in relation to its command.

We could develop further our discussion of capital as a parasitic function. But for now, I only want to develop it in positive terms, recalling the importance of general intellect in bringing about the surplus of social production. The point is that productive force emerges from subjects and is organized in cooperation. In the age of general intellect, productive cooperation is thus not imposed by capital but is, rather, a capacity of immaterial labour power, of the mental labour that cannot be other than cooperative, and therefore of linguistic labour, which equally inevitably has to express itself in cooperative forms. Capitalist development has, so to speak, brought us to a point where a *new primitive accumulation* has come about, an accumulation to which general intellect itself becomes the key. What characterizes this situation is the fact that labour power, now intellectualized or at any rate immaterialized, expands (within primitive accumulation) as an epidemic, including in its development also those who are formally external to it. This brings to mind an excellent Ph.D. which I supervised in Paris, on digital primitive accumulation in the Mexican south of California. The process described was that of a total change in the productive paradigm as a result of the early spread of the computer industry. At first sight it appeared that what was happening was an expansion of the capitalist market and the formation of areas of production of poverty in terms of unequal exchange (between American California and Mexican California): in fact, the process was the opposite, namely that *chicanos*, who until the day before had been picking peas and oranges and were now beginning to screw in microchips, *also* began to destroy every line of exclusion, to spill over every border, and to extend over the entire labour market, on their own initiative, impulses and tendencies towards self-valorization. We are thus seeing a real and actual digital primitive accumulation, which, however, in comparison to industrial primitive accumulation, saw capitalist command being kept relatively on the outside of the areas of production, and the force of cooperation expanding itself spontaneously on every hand.

If this is a fair description of the situation in which we now find ourselves, our question then becomes: what is method and how can it act within this real condition (assuming that such a thing as an autonomy of method still exists)? Obviously the independence that we can assume for method at this point is very relative, supposing that a minimum of externality, 'outsideness', is still available to it. In fact, if method is an activity of knowledge (as it seems logical to accept), it should now be part of the mode of production, it should be internal to it. At the same moment that we construct it and thereby produce knowledge, in that same way we produce commodities. We answer the question of how method can be defined by saying that it becomes evident only when the non-productive emerges, that is, when there is blockage of cognitive–productive activity, interruption of informational processes and, in general, anything that arrests the movements of consciousness, cooperation and language. It is thus only at the moment in which the capture of social value is interrupted, when capital is forced to block processes of production in order to continue to exist – it is only then that value shows its social, independent force (and the method, from within the process, presents it for our consideration). We are by now so far from a description of capital as a progressive force that we can understand how capital, in order to exist, is forced to block the processes of social capture of value, because these are excedent, going beyond its capacity of command. The concept of method which stands behind this argument confronts us with the fact (reveals it, demonstrates it) that *the transformation of labour into cognitive activity is characterized by an extreme excess of valorization*: an excedence of knowledge relative to its product. Method is part of this excedence, and conquers its own relative independence within this surplus. If knowledge is put into production, the productivity of this labour will bring about, in addition to a further increase of wealth, further knowledge as well. One example which clarifies what I am saying is the crisis of the *net-economy*, that is, the fact that the totality of informatic and informational systems fails to keep up with the surplus of curiosity, of cognitive *potenza*. Now, what I am saying here, from an ontological point of view, is that there really is a change of paradigm, a change of the general model on which capitalism is organized. If this is true, let us repeat our question: how might a new *Einleitung* on method be possible?

So let us try again to answer this question and offer some elements of a new methodological introduction on the basis of what has been said thus far. It is interesting to stress that the criticism we insistently make of Marx is far from separating ourselves from the structure of his reasoning, or from the basic categories of what he is saying: rather, it questions them in order to perfect them. *Our critique actively embraces the Marxian point of view*. In effect, the transformations taking place in the world of work, which are changing the whole paradigmatic picture, do not remove labour from its creative frame of being and history; they simply establish that labour is altering, changing and increasingly becoming *cogni-*

tive activity. Another fundamental element, as regards continuity with Marx's thinking, is that this labour continues to be, in our experience, *exploited labour.* At this point it would be worth restating the two premises of Marx's ontology. The first premise is that the world is created by labour. The second is that this labour will always will be exploited for as long as capitalism exists. Therefore we must focus our analysis, on the one hand, on the forces of labour that construct the world, and on the other on the possibility of liberating labour from exploitation. (What exploitation is, we already saw when we referred to the suspension of development, which can present itself in absolute terms – as crisis – or following the ever-diverse and always diversely functional hierarchical modulations of capitalist command over the world-wide market.)

Behind the decision to discuss ontology there lies not only the banal insistence on the affirmation that, for materialism, being is what it is and that therefore you cannot invent the real; there is also the attempt to address, within this discussion, a philosophical perception of being, in a constitutive key, matched to that alternative theory of materialism within modernity which was typical, for instance, of *Spinozism.* This enables us to think method within an imaginary of the liberation of being; a method which, taking as given the expulsion of all transcendence, of every outside, from this world-stage, rediscovers in humanity the ability to produce, to construct the world in an independent way, and therefore to project therein the values through which people live and produce. This materialist or radically immanentist affirmation is present in our approach to method – an approach which teaches us to move between the productive and the product, between the concrete and the abstract, between the subjective and the objective, between the constructive and the instituted. What is important in these pairings is the *within,* which in the postmodern dimension of production reveals itself to be the exclusive terrain of analysis.

In the second place, the method has to permit us to integrate its scientific and operative determinations *within the concept of living labour*; or, better, we need to be in a position to define *method* immediately *as living labour* in terms of knowledge; so that the production process that derives from it is open to the kind of positive hybridization that intellectuality proposes to every production. That is to say that the method will follow the transformation of labour from the inside, always, in each of its figures.

In the third place, at the centre of its analysis method must reconsider the concept and the reality of exploitation. If *exploitation* by now offers variants outside of every preconstituted law and offers itself as a variable function between the expropriation of productive cooperation and its hierarchization, between linguistic labour and normalization of systems, capital, in exploiting labour, determines several kinds of *exclusion*. Thinking in terms of the extension of knowledge and of active knowing, of its exuberance and its excedence of value, means thinking in terms of an explosive topography of mental labour, but also in terms of the attempt by capital to block its *potenza*. Empire constructs a politics of global apartheid as capacity for subdividing, blocking and subordinating the capacity to express value at all levels. Imperial exploitation becomes this machine, which is very different from capitalist and imperialist exploitation in the age of competition.

To end on this point. When we deal with the reactivity of subjects implicated in exploitation, method must enable us to stand within the wholeness of the process. In particular, it must integrate cooperative determinations and, at the same time, succeed in grasping the immediate and continuous excedence of knowledge (which probably – but we shall see this later – is also called *resistance*).

The continuous and transformative causality of the social movements *enters into* the concept of capital, and does so increasingly tightly. These movements no longer have an outside, but are located within the framework of capital. The lived is traversed by different accumulations and praxes; it is the result of their dynamics and in the end it discovers itself in *the biopolitical dimension*, that is, in a *dispositif* which is no longer tied only to production, but, obviously, to the whole of life. We arrive at this conclusion methodically, in other words not from the outside, by saying for example that capital has occupied the whole of life, *but from within*: it is labour that has occupied the whole of life. And it is both exploited labour and intelligent labour. (In this regard, we often come across a polemic that would be worth restating here. When people speak of immaterial labour and identify it in the higher productive forms organized by language or affective nexuses and the like, what is generally expressed is an over-idealistic or over-psychologizing conception of these processes. This leads tomethodological difficulties – in particular that of excluding the possibility of hybridization between material and immaterial labour: the former, as it gradually develops, is drawn within the second; in other words, by transforming it, it creates a situation in which material labour is increasingly within intellectual and immaterial labour. It suffices to think, for example, of the paradoxes involved in peasant labour, into which the new technologies are introducing more and more elements of immaterial labour . . .)

Proceeding in our methodological endeavour, we now need to consider *the definition of biopolitics*, starting from how it appears in Foucault. The term refers to the way in which, between the end of the eighteenth and the start of the nineteenth century, power tends to govern not only individuals through a number of disciplinary processes, but also the ensemble of living people, which are thus constituted as populations. The biopolitical, through localized biopowers, concerns itself with the management of health, hygiene, nutrition, sexuality and fertility, to the extent that these topics become matters of importance for power in the development of the modern state. In developing this part of the Lesson I follow the summaries offered by Judith Revel.

Foucault moves from a historical observation, namely from the fact that, starting with the classic age of the French absolute monarchy, power began to be interested in populations, in the sense of concerning itself in general terms with their reproduction (reproduction understood as health, hygiene, nutrition, and so on). The notion of biopolitics thus implies a historical analysis of the political and functional rationality of government in the era in which it appears. In this particular instance, the historical reflection relates to the birth of *liberalism*, where by liberalism, still in Foucauldian terms, we understand an exercise of government that does not limit itself to maximizing the effects of appropriation (and thus reducing its costs), but above all something characterized by the risk of governing too much. While the state of absolute monarchy, in the classical age, had developed power through a growth of its own functions, the liberal reflection, according to Foucault, does not start from the existence of the state in order to find in government the means to achieve its own ends, but from society, that is, from a complex relationship of internality and externality to the state. This form of governing (or of governability) is not reducible either to a pure juridical analysis, understood as a mechanism of production and interpretation of norms, or to an economic reading of, for example, the Marxist type. The new science of government (which also includes juridical and economic functions) presents itself rather as *a technology of power* that has the population as its object, and which thus invests the different forms into which the population is organized. Now, from this perspective, the population is an ensemble of coexisting living beings who present particular ontological/biological features and whose life is susceptible of being controlled with the aim of guaranteeing, via a better management of labour power, an ordered growth of society.

In a talk given at the University of Bahia in 1978, Foucault proposed that 'the discovery of population and, at the same time, the discovery of the individual and the trainable [dressable] manipulable body present themselves as a specific technological nucleus around which the political processes of the West were transformed. That moment saw the invention of that which, in parallel to anatomo-politics, is known as bio politics.' Taking up from Foucault, we need to highlight *the transition of the art of governing from discipline to control*. By discipline we mean a form of government of, or over, individuals in a singular and repetitive way. Updating the definition to our own time, we could say that discipline is that which covers the entirety of the fabric of society, through the Taylorization of labour, the Fordist forms of solicitation of, and the wage-based control of, consumption, through to the organization in macroeconomic forms of Keynesian policies. By control, on the other hand, we mean the government of populations through mechanisms which collectively invest labour, the imaginary, and life itself. Here too, speaking of our own times, we can say that the transition from discipline to control is today represented by *the transition from Fordism to post-Fordism*. In Foucauldian terms, we can say that in the post-Fordist phase control passes more through television than through the discipline of the factory, through the imaginary and the mind rather than through direct discipline exercised over bodies. Defined in these terms, in opposition to anatomo-politics (technologies of training and taming of the individual and the body), biopolitics thus marks the transition from discipline as control over the bodies of individuals to control as a technology of power exercised over populations. While discipline was an anatomo-politics of the body and was applied essentially to individuals, the biopolitical is, rather, a great social medicine, which is applied to the population with the aim of governing its life. *Life itself is now part of the operating terrain of power.*

The notion of biopolitics raises various problems. The first relates to a contradiction that we find in Foucault himself. In the first texts where the term appears, it seems to be tied to that of 'police science', in other words to the science of the maintenance of social order. From this point of view, biopolitics, as a police science, lies at the basis of administrative science and grows together with it in the history of public law. Later on, however, biopolitics seems, on the contrary, to mark the moment of surpassing public law, and therefore every political function that lies within the traditional state–society dichotomy. What we then have is a political economy of life in general. Whereas at the start, biopolitics is born as a police science, as a technology tied to the action of the state, subsequently it comes to be a general fabric that covers the entire relationship between state and society. However, another problem arises from this second formulation: *should we think of biopolitics as an ensemble of biopowers that derive from the activity of government or, on the contrary, can we say that, to the extent that power has invested the whole of life, thus life too becomes a power* [potere]? Better still, can we say that biopolitics is a power expressed by life itself, not only in labour and in language, but also in bodies, in affects, desires and sexuality? Can we identify, within life itself, the place of emergence of a sort of counter-power, of a *potenza*, a production of subjectivity that exists as a moment of de-subjectification? In this second perspective, in other words where life presents itself as *potenza*, the notion of biopolitics would be fundamental for a reformulation of the political relationship: the biopolitical would represent the transition from the political to the ethical, or rather a perspective for constructing an ethics of the body, of the life of pleasures and of the life of labour. In 1982, Foucault maintained that analysis of the population, the questioning of relations of power and of the antagonism between relations of power and the affirmation of the intransigence of freedom, can be seen as an ever-ongoing political task. It is there, in that intransigent opening of freedom against every machine, against every structure of power, that there is established the political task inherent to every social existence. (See 'Subject and power', in *Michel Foucault: Beyond Structuralism and Hermeneutics*, ed. H. Dreyfus and P. Rabinow, University of Chicago Press, Chicago, 1982.)

Thus we have seen how the concept of biopolitics is born and how it is located within contemporary scientific experience. It is located in the dynamic that runs from the historical identification of the extension of powers of the state in modernity (in concomitance with the ever deeper and wider government of populations) through to a moment in which this relation is overturned. It is around this overturning that a series of Foucauldian researchers began to propose a *distinction between biopower and the biopolitical*. We speak of biopower when the state expresses command over life through its technologies and its mechanisms of power; but we speak of the biopolitical when the critical analysis of command is done from the viewpoint of experiences of subjectivation and freedom, in short, so to speak, from the bottom. Biopower, from this point of view, is the highest characterization of the capitalist modernization of social relationships. It is here, in effect, that the areas of capitalist development and those of social development overlap. On the other hand, from the point of view of social ontology, what seems more interesting today is the definition of the biopolitical, in other words the emergence of subjectivity. This is not only a break in methodological considerations; it is also the perception of an ontological opening of the liberation of processes which are moving in all directions. Below, in concluding these observations, we shall see how, within these processes, one can properly begin to speak of the production of subjectivity.

But first let us examine the difference between biopower and the biopolitical. We use the term *biopower* to identify the big structures and functions of power; we use the term *biopolitical context* or *biopolitics* to refer to the spaces in which relations, struggles and productions of power are developed. We speak of *biopower* when thinking of the sources or wellsprings of state power, and the specific technologies that the state produces, for example, in order to control populations; we speak of *biopolitics* or the *biopolitical context* when referring to the complex of resistances, and occasions and measures of the clash between social *dispositifs* of power. However, we need to be very careful in characterizing the micro-conflictual spaces or Foucauldian micropolitics: they are not circuits in indifference, but rather circuits that determine lines of flight in terms which are sometimes absolute . . . In short, in these spaces difference is not dispersed, indeed, *when we speak about the biopolitical we are speaking above all of strong fabrics.* I emphasize this, because in Italy the arrival of these ideas took place under the influence of so-called 'weak thought' (*pensiero debole*) in the early 1980s, and therefore these concepts and methods were defined in direct polemic with class conflicts and their production. In France things were even worse, because both before and after the death of Foucault these ideas were taken over by the *nouveaux philosophes*, and when they were not they were promoted by the right (for example by François Ewald) in the area of the 'bio-politics of risk': *soft* biopolitics became a fundamental weapon *against* social welfare practices. I remind the reader of all this in order to emphasize a basic methodological point: concepts go around and come around, and it is always good to specify them in relation to the structure of meaning that connotes them genea-logically. From this point of view, *biopolitics is an extension of the class struggle.*

Now, let us see if we can add further elements to our analysis of the genesis of the biopolitical. We pointed out previously how important it was to translate into physical and material forms the figure of general intellect. In this perspective, Christian Marazzi's book *Il posto dei calzini* [*The Place Where the Socks Go*] was very important. Here the paradox of the so-called non-labour of women is described: a non-labour which is so pervasive that there is no place in life (starting from the place where the family's most inti-mate objects are kept) which is not occupied by it. And it is there, in this non-labour, that a truly vital truth is offered up, precisely in the 'place where the socks are kept': it is recognized as a characteristic and central place, not of non-labour, but of *new* productive labour, which consists of knowledge (where the socks go), but, above all, of affect, of relations that may be servile or free, but which are played out entirely within this context. All this has great relevance, in attempting to define biopolitics, to the realities in which we live, and which are described in useful ways by Marazzi. If we wanted to go further in trying to define bio-politics, we might also pick up points from Deleuze and Guattari, where biopolitics arises out of the totality of affective labour, of relational labour, of the temporal flexibility and spatial mobility of labour: these elements now become characteristic of the new quality of labour that characterizes our present era.

There is, then, another point to be made regarding biopolitics. It relates to the *embodiment* of general intellect and to those dimensions of precariousness, flexibility and mobility of labour that we have highlighted thus far. Now, these dimensions have to do with *anthropological transformations* imposed by biopolitical development; they fix a relationship between biopolitics and anthropology. Again, we need only think of the transformations of labour. In the history of labour (of its evolution) there have been changes that we can see as sometimes progressive and at other times regressive. Take, for example, the transition from the skilled worker of the first disciplinary phase of capitalist develop-ment to the mass worker of the second phase, a transition we have dealt with extensively. From a certain point of view this was a regressive anthropological development, for instance when one considers the capacity of the mass worker to control labour processes (now reduced to virtually nil, whereas it had been sub-stantial in the case of the skilled worker); at the same time, however, there was also a positive evolution in the abstraction of labour, and this saw the emergence of the ability of the worker to work everywhere, to apply himself/ herself to a whole range of working activities. A passive ability, to be sure, but one which brought with it a positive abstraction and the formation of a new degree of *potenza*. The possibility of passing from one sector of production to another, and the new mobility, began to configure themselves as a way of conceiving life, and sometimes of enjoying and constructing new spaces and new temporalities of labour. This is biopolitics in a most concrete sense, with never-ending grounds for analysis.

Let us take a look at other consequences of these presupposi-tions. The first consequence lies in the steps towards a *unification of labour* which are implicit in these processes. What we see is that the whole labour process is tending *towards immaterial labour*. In some respects, immaterial labour is abstract labour in its higher expression. Our discussion of Empire would have been impossible if it had not started from these premises. It is only by taking these premises as our starting point that we were able to dislodge pre-constituted definitions of labour that gave us static configurations of movements and struggles. Our primary biopolitical perception of Empire is thus rooted in the development of mobility of labour, of the great processes of emigration, the great biopolitical movements. These movements are not simply negative, they do not only represent flights from poverty or from tyranny, but *they are also movements which move positively in search of freedom*, towards wealth, employment, invention, towards the centrality of immaterial labour and which reveal a great desire to enter into these circuits. The second consequence relates to *poverty*. How are we to qualify poverty today? First we should have one thing clear: poverty has always been viewed with a certain contempt in the communist tradition. The poor were always seen as potential enemies of the working class, since they were viewed as an 'industrial reserve army'. But such worries no longer apply. We know, in fact, that today *poverty is the simple fact of not being able to make your activity worth something.* Thus even the poor migrant or the excluded is someone who has a *potenza* to express. If we develop this argument, we could thus recognize that the poor are the salt of the earth, because they are a general activity, a *potenza* thus far unresolved and blocked. If the function of exploitation is to deprive people of breath, space and mobility, as well as of the capacity for cooperation and creation of value, then the poor person is not only excluded but is also an exemplary subject of exploitation. In this sense the poor person and the worker must struggle together.

To put it another way, the poor do not stand outside of history; there is nothing that it is outside production, we are all here on the inside. So this non-place which is the outside – exclusion, the place of poverty – cannot itself exist without resistance: this is the elementary concept that I want to present here. *The exodus from poverty thus consists in struggling, exactly as workers struggle, in order to destroy capitalist power.* Here we need to discuss and deepen these questions in order to make them our own . . . I am talking particularly to people of my own age, whose experience has always been that of labour and its defence. It is not at all utopian – this we must understand – to move also outside of organized labour. But this does not mean outside of capitalist development . . . The alternative that we propose in terms of a common struggle of workers and the poor is not a mythical alternative, because it constructs a struggle that runs through the whole of life, and constructs subjectivity . . . Certainly, if labour had remained purely material labour, all this could appear dubious: but it is not, because labour is by now production of the brain, and all of us have a brain. Perhaps at this point one could say that, in the case of the poor (and of this poverty which, here, begins to present itself as a positive force), we also have the collapse of the last figure of the progressive function of capital. The *poor person*, 'free as a bird', *here becomes the paradigm of the worker*. It was Marx who defined the worker, who was the precondition of primitive capitalist accumulation, as 'free as a bird'. He meant also as poor as a bird. But it is beginning from this poverty, precisely here, on the borderline that divides us from death, that everything begins.

So, to summarize what has been said in this second lesson, we have addressed the reversal of the relationship between matter and method that emerged at the end of Lesson 1. In Marx's Einleitung *to the* Grundrisse *(as I interpreted it in my* Marx beyond Marx, *above.) we discover that method is based on social ontology. Once we recognize ourselves as being in a situation in which immaterial labour (intellectual, and so on) has established a hegemony over material labour (industrial labour, and so on) we need a new methodological* Einleitung *in order to be able to interpret the reality around us.*

The interpretation of the 'Fragment on machines' in Marx's Grundrisse *allowed us, via various interpretations, to come close to an ontological definition of the new methodological phase. We owe to Carlo Vercellone, Antonella Corsani and Maurizio Lazzarato (see their writings in the journals* Posse *(Manifestolibri, Rome), and* Multitudes *(Exils, Paris)) a series of interpretations which all tend to assign to the definition of general intellect a change of paradigm within the process of industrial production.*

Once we assume the hegemony of the new model, there follow consequences related to the position of the researcher in the analysis. In particular, once we have the real subsumption of society within capital, it is clear that the definition of methodology has to place itself within development (and therefore outside of every reference to preconstituted or naturalistic values, that is, to a natural foundation). In this area Michael Hardt and I have developed a broad methodological approach in our Multitude: War and Democracy in the Age of Empire, *Penguin Books, London, 2005. But having reached this point we need to go further. We need to pursue the* methodological inquiry not merely in analytical terms, but also in constitutive terms. *This means that our analysis must deepen to the point of setting in motion its own ontological base – in other words, set its actors in motion no longer simply as (productive)* mental powers, but also as bodies. *Here we are at the centre of the transition to the biopolitical, the biopolitical embodiment of method, or, better, the biopolitical figuration of general intellect. I believe that Christian Marazzi, in his writings ranging from* Il posto dei calzini *(The Place of the Socks) (Boringhieri, Turin, 1999) to* Capitale e linguaggio *(Capital and Language) (Rubbettino, Soveria Mannelli 2001), is the writer who has best addressed this paradigmatic shift of method towards taking biopolitical dimensions.*

As for the internal analysis of biopolitics and the division between biopolitics and biopower, as well as for the distinction between disciplinary regimes and regimes of control, the basic text is of course Foucault *by Gilles Deleuze, published in 1985 (Minuit, Paris; Cronopio, Naples, 2002). See also Judith Revel,* Vocabulaire de Foucault *(Ellipses, Paris, 2002). And for further material on biopolitics and the metamorphosis of bodies, see my articles published in the collection* Desiderio del mostro *(Desire of the Monster), Manifestolibri, Rome, 2001.*

6

Globalization and Democracy

Michael Hardt and Antonio Negri

et interrogabat eum quod tibi nomen est et dicit ei legio nomen mihi est quia multi sumus [And [Jesus] asked him, what is thy name? And he answered, saying, my name is legion: for we are many].

Gospel according to St Mark 5: 9

The dominant modern notion of democracy has been intimately tied to the nation-state. To investigate the contemporary status of democracy, then, we should look first at the changing powers and role of the nation-state. Many theorists claim, and many others contest, that the diverse phenomena commonly grouped under the term 'globalization' have eroded, or even negated, the powers of nation-states.[1] Too often, however, this is advanced as an either/or proposition: either nation-states are still important or there is a new global order. Both, in fact, are true. The era of globalization has not brought the end of the nation-state – nation-states still fulfill extremely important functions in the establishment and regulation of economic, political, and cultural norms – but nation-

[1] The most detailed and influential argument that globalization has not undermined the powers of nation-states and that globalization is in this sense a myth is presented by Paul Hirst and Grahame Thompson, *Globalization in Question: The International Economy and the Possibilities of Governance*, 2nd edn (Polity Press, Cambridge, 1999).

states have indeed been displaced from the position of sovereign authority. A focus on the concept and practices of sovereignty helps to clarify this discussion.

We propose the concept of Empire to name our contemporary global arrangement. Empire refers above all to a new form of sovereignty that has succeeded the sovereignty of the nation-state, an unlimited form of sovereignty that knows no boundaries or, rather, knows only flexible, mobile boundaries. We borrow the concept of Empire from the ancient Roman figure, in which Empire is seen to supersede the alternation of the three classical forms of government – monarchy, aristocracy and democracy – by combining them in a single sovereign rule. Our contemporary Empire is indeed monarchical, and this is most apparent in times of military conflict when we can see the extent to which the Pentagon, with its atomic weapons and superior military technology, effectively rules the world. The supra-national economic institutions, such as the WTO, the World Bank, and the IMF, also at times exercise a monarchical rule over global affairs. Our Empire, however, is also aristocratic, that is, ruled by a limited group of élite actors. The power of nation-states is central here, because the few dominant nation-states manage to govern global economic and cultural flows through a kind of aristocratic rule. This aristocracy of nations is revealed clearly, for example, when the G8 nations meet or when the UN Security Council exercises its authority. The major transnational corporations too, in concert and in conflict, constitute a form of aristocracy. Finally, Empire is also democratic in the sense that it claims to represent the global people, although, as we will argue below, this claim to representation is largely illusory. The entire group of nation-states, the dominant and the subordinated ones together, fulfil the primary role here to the extent that they are assumed in some way to represent their peoples. The UN General Assembly is perhaps the most prominent symbol of this democracy of nations. When we recognize that nation-states do not in fact adequately represent their peoples, however, we can have recourse to non-governmental organizations as the democratic or representative institutions. The functioning of the various kinds of NGOs as democratic or representative mechanisms is a very complex and important question, which we should not pretend to treat adequately here. In short, Empire is a single sovereign subject that comprehends within its logic all three of these classical forms or levels of rule, the monarchic, the aristocratic, and the democratic. Empire, in other words, is a distinctive form of sovereignty on account of its ability to include and manage difference within its constitution.

From this perspective we can see that the functions and authority of nation-states have not disappeared. It is probably more accurate to say that the primary functions of nation-states – the regulation of currencies, economic flows, population migrations, legal norms, cultural values, and so forth – have maintained their importance but have been transformed through the contemporary processes of globalization. The radical qualitative shift should be recognized rather in terms of sovereignty. Nation-states can no longer claim the role of sovereign or ultimate authority, as they could in the modern era. Empire now stands above the nation-states, as the final authority, and indeed presents a new form of sovereignty.

We should point out that this is a major historical shift only from the perspective of the dominant nation-states. The subordinate nations were never really sovereign. The entry into modernity, for many nation-states, was the entry into relations of economic and political subordination that undercut any sovereignty to which the nation might pretend. This shift in the form of sovereignty – from the modern sovereignty located in the nation-state to our postmodern imperial sovereignty – nonetheless affects us all. Even where national sovereignty was never a reality, the passage to Empire has transformed our forms of thought and the range of our political possibilities. In the light of Empire we have to reconsider and re-conceive all the key concepts of political philosophy.

Democracy unrealized, democracy unrealizable

This brings us back, first and foremost, to the concept of democracy. The dominant modern notion of democracy was, as we claimed at the outset, based on representational institutions and structures within the bounded national space and dependent on national sovereignty.[2] What was represented in the democratic

---

[2] This is the fundamental argument of David Held, *Democracy and the Global Order: From the modern state to cosmopolitan governance* (Stanford University Press, Stanford, 1995).

national institutions was the people, and hence modern national sovereignty tended to take the form of popular sovereignty. In other words, the claim that the nation was sovereign tended to become identical with the claim that the people was sovereign. But what, or who, is the people? The people is not a natural or empirical entity; one cannot arrive at the identity of the people by summing up, or even averaging, the entire population. The people, rather, is a form of *representation* that makes of the population a unity. Three elements are centrally important here. First of all, the people is one, as Hobbes and the entire modern tradition often repeated. The people can be sovereign only as an identity, a unity. Secondly, the key to the construction of the people is representation. The empirical multiplicity of the population is made an identity through mechanisms of representation – and here we should include both the political and the aesthetic connotations of the term 'representation'. Finally, these mechanisms of representation are based on a notion and on a condition of measure – and by measure here we mean not so much a quantifiable condition but as a bounded one. A bounded or measured multiplicity can be represented as a unity; but the non-measurable, the boundless cannot be represented. This is one sense in which the notion of the people is intimately tied to the bounded national space. In short, the people is not an immediate nor an eternal identity, but rather the result of a complex process, which is proper to a specific social formation and historical period.

We can simplify this complex situation for a moment and consider only the institutional, political mechanisms of representation, of which the electoral process was, at least ideologically, the most important one. The notion of 'one person, one vote', for example, was one of the ideals towards which the various modern schemata of popular representation and sovereignty tended. There is no need for us to argue here that these schemata of popular representation have always been imperfect and in fact largely illusory. There have long been important critiques of the mechanisms of popular representation in modern democratic societies. It is perhaps an exaggeration to characterize elections as an opportunity to choose which member of the ruling class will misrepresent the people for the next two, four, or six years, but there is certainly some truth in it too, and low voter turnout is undoubtedly a symptom of the crisis of popular representation through electoral institutions. We think that today, however, popular representation is undermined in a more basic and fundamental way.

In the passage to Empire, national space loses its definition, national boundaries (although still important) are relativized, and even national imaginaries are destabilized. As national sovereignty is displaced by the authority of the new supra-national power, Empire, political reality loses its measure. In this situation, the impossibility of representing the people becomes increasingly clear, and thus the concept of the people itself tends to evaporate.

From an institutional, political perspective, imperial sovereignty conflicts with, and even negates, any conception of popular sovereignty. Consider, for example, the functioning of the supra-national economic institutions such as the World Bank, the IMF, and the WTO. To a large extent, the conditionality required by these institutions takes out of the hands of nation-states decisions over economic and social policy. The subordinate nation-states most visibly, but also the dominant ones, are subject to the rule of these institutions.[3] It is clear that these supra-national economic institutions do not and cannot represent the people, except in the most distant and abstract sense – in the sense, for example, that some nation-states, which in some way represent their peoples, designate representatives to the institutions. If one looks for representation in such institutions, there will always inevitably remain a 'democratic deficit'. Which means that, in

---

[3] Many authors characterize and lament this shift in decision-making from national to supra-national institutions as the increasing domination of the economic over the political (on the assumption that the nation-state is the only context in which politics can be conducted). Several of these authors invoke the work of Karl Polanyi in their attempt to re-embed economic markets within social markets. See, for example, James H. Mittleman, *The Globalization Syndrome: Transformations and Resistance* (Princeton University Press, Princeton, NJ, 2000), and John Gray, *False Dawn: The Delusions of Global Capitalism* (The New Press, New York, 1998). In our view it is a mistake to separate the economic and the political in this way and to insist on the autonomy of the political. The supra-national economic institutions are also political institutions themselves. The fundamental difference is that these institutions do not allow for (even the pretence of) popular representation.

our view, it is no accident that these institutions are so isolated from popular representation. They function precisely to the extent that they are excluded from the mechanisms of popular representation.

Some of the best liberal Euro-American theorists of globalization do in fact argue that we need to reform the global system and to reinforce the mechanisms of democratic political rule, but even they do not imagine that such supra-national institutions could ever become representative in any popular sense. One of the fundamental obstacles is the problem of determining what or who is the people in such a conception. One would presumably have to develop a notion of the global people that extends beyond any national or ethnic conception, to unite the entirety of humanity, a challenge which falls well outside the purpose of all these liberal theorizations!

What, then, does constitute democratic reform in the views of the various leading liberal reformers such as Robert Keohane, Joseph Stiglitz, David Held, Richard Falk and Ulrick Beck? It is striking in fact how widespread is the use of the term 'democracy' in this literature and how universally accepted it is as a goal. One major component of democratic reform is, simply, greater transparency – *glasnost* and *perestroika*; perhaps we should understand this as a Gorbachev project for the age of globalization. Transparency itself, however, is not democracy and does not constitute representation. A more substantive notion, omnipresent in the literature, is that of 'accountability' (which is often paired with the notion of 'governance'). The concept of accountability could refer to mechanisms of popular representation, but in these discourses it does not. One has to ask 'accountable to whom?', and then we find that the reformers do not propose making global institutions accountable to a global (or even a national) people – the people, precisely, is missing. Rather, the reform would involve making the global institutions accountable to other institutions, and especially to a community of experts. If the IMF were more transparent and accountable to economic experts, for example, there would be safeguards against its implementing disastrous policies, such as those dictated by the IMF in South-East Asia in the late 1990s. What is central and most interesting about the use of the terms 'accountability' and 'governance' in these discussions, however, is that these terms straddle so comfortably the political and the economic realms. Accountability and governance have long been central concepts in the theoretical vocabulary of capitalist corporations.[4] The notions of accountability and governance seem to be directed most clearly at assuring economic efficiency and stability, not at constructing any popular or representational form of democratic control. Finally, although the term 'democracy' is omnipresent in the literature, no global version of democracy in its modern liberal form – that is, as popular representation – is even on the agenda. It seems, in fact, that the greatest conceptual obstacle that prevents these theorists from imagining a global representative schema is precisely the notion of the people. Who is the global people? It seems impossible today to grasp the people as a political subject and, moreover, to represent it institutionally.[5]

We have thought it important to dwell so long on the question of the democratic reform of these institutions, not only in order to take seriously the arguments of the reformist theorists but also, and more importantly, because this discourse can be found so widely among various factions of the protest movements against the WTO, the World Bank and the IMF. Groups call for greater inclusion and representation in the decision-making process of the institutions themselves, demanding, for example, trade union representation, NGO representation or the like. Such demands may have some positive results, but they ultimately face insurmountable obstacles. Our argument casts all this on a much more general plane. If we conceive of democracy in terms of a sovereign authority representative of the people, then democracy in the imperial age is not only unrealized, but actually unrealizable.

---

[4] We are indebted to Craig Borowiak for his analyses of the concept of accountability in the contemporary globalization discussion.

[5] From this perspective, the project for the construction of a political Europe can appear to some as the solution to the puzzle of democracy in the age of globalization. The hypothesis is that the continent can substitute for the nation and revive the mechanisms of representational democracy. This seems to us, however, a false solution. Even if one could represent institutionally the European people as a coherent subject, a political Europe is not capable of claiming sovereign authority. Regional powers, like nation-states, are merely elements which function within the ultimate sovereignty of Empire.

Democracy of the multitude

Thus we have to explore new forms of democracy, forms that are non-representative or differently representative, to discover a democracy which is adequate to our own times. We have already argued that the modern notion of democracy is intimately tied to national sovereignty and to a fixed national space – in short, that the modern notion is founded on measure. Now we should turn our attention back to explore further the other element in the equation, the people. The people, as we said earlier, is a product of representation. In modern political theory, the people is most strongly configured as the product of the founding contractual act of bourgeois society, as all the modern liberal theorists explain, from Hobbes to Rawls. The contract makes of the population a united social body. This contractual act is, however, nonexistent, mystificatory and outdated. The contract is nonexistent in the sense that no anthropological or historical fact allows us to assume its reality; rather, the contract negates any memory of its foundation, and this is certainly part of its violence: its fundamental denial of difference. Secondly, the contract is mystificatory in the sense that the people it constructs is presented as equal when the subjects who form it are in fact unequal; the concepts of justice and legitimacy that ground it serve only the strongest, who exercise a force of domination and exploitation on the rest of the population. This concept of a people formed through the contract is outdated, finally, because it looks to a society forged by capital: contractualism, people and capitalism function in fact to make of the plurality a unity, to make of differences a homologous totality, to make of the wealth of all the singular lives in the population the poverty of some and the power of others. But this no longer works: it used to work as long as labour, needs and desires were so miserable that they received the command of capital as a welcome comfort and a source of security when faced with the risks of the construction of value, the liberation of the imagination, and the organization of society. Today, however, the terms have changed. It is rather our monstrous intelligence and our cooperative power that are put in play: we are a multitude of powerful subjects, a multitude of intelligent monsters.

We thus need to shift our conceptual focus from the people to the multitude. The multitude cannot be grasped in the terms of contractualism – and, in general, in the terms of a transcendental philosophy. In the most general sense, the multitude defies representation because it is a multiplicity, indefinite and unmeasurable. The people is represented as a unity, but the multitude is not representable because it is monstrous in relation to the teleological and transcendental rationalisms of modernity. In contrast to the concept of the people, the concept of multitude is a singular multiplicity, a concrete universal. The people constituted a social body, but the multitude does not – the multitude is the flesh of life. If on the one side we contrast the multitude with the people, on the other side we should contrast it with the masses or the mob. The masses and the mob are most often used to name an irrational and passive social force, dangerous and violent precisely because so easily manipulated. The multitude, in contrast, is an active social agent – a multiplicity that acts. The multitude is not a unity, as is the people, but, in contrast to the masses and the mob, we can see that it is organized. It is an active, self-organizing agent. One great advantage of the concept of multitude is that it displaces all the modern arguments based on the fear of the masses, and even those about the tyranny of the majority, which have so often served as a kind of blackmail to force us to accept, and even to call for, a power to dominate us.

From the perspective of power, however, what can be done with the multitude? In effect, there is nothing to do with it, because the nexus among the unity of the subject (people), the form of its composition (contract among individuals), and the mode of government (monarchy, aristocracy and democracy, separate or combined) has been blown apart. The radical modification of the mode of production through the hegemony of immaterial labour power and through cooperative living labour – this ontological, productive, biopolitical revolution – has overturned the parameters of 'good government' and destroyed the modern idea of a community that functions for capitalist accumulation, as capitalism imagined it from the beginning.

Allow us a brief parenthesis. Between the fifteenth and sixteenth centuries, when modernity appeared in the form of a revolution, the revolutionaries imagined themselves as monsters. Gargantua and Pantagruel can serve as emblems for all the giants and extreme figures of freedom and invention that have come down to us through the ages and proposed the gigantic task of becoming more free. Today we need new giants and new monsters to bring together nature and history, labour and politics, art and invention, so as to demonstrate the new power that the birth of 'general intellect', the hegemony of immaterial labour, the new passions of the abstract activity of the multitude provide to humanity. We need a new Rabelais – or, really, several.

Spinoza and Marx spoke of the democracy of the multitude or, rather, of a form of democracy that no longer has anything to do with the democracy which, along with monarchy and aristocracy, constitutes one of the classical forms of government. The democracy which Spinoza advocates is what he calls an *absolute* democracy – absolute in the sense of being without limit and without measure. The conceptions of social contracts and bounded social bodies are thus completely cast aside. When we say that absolute democracy is outside of the theory (and the mystificatory practice) of the classical forms of government, we mean also, obviously, that any attempt to realize democracy through the reform of the imperial institutions will be vain and useless. We mean, furthermore, that the only path to realize a democracy of the multitude is the path of revolution. What does it mean, however, to call for a revolutionary democracy adequate to the imperial world? Up to this point, we have simply focused on what it is not. It is no longer something that depends on the concept of nation (on the contrary, it is increasingly defined by the struggle against the nation). We have also seen that it is something that does not correspond to the concept of the people, and in fact is opposed to any attempt to present as unitary what is different. We need at this point to look to other concepts in order to get some help in understanding a democracy of the multitude. The concept of counterpower seems fundamental to us when we deal with these new contents of the absolute democracy of the multitude.

Modern counterpower and the paradoxes
of modern insurrection

The concept of counterpower consists primarily of three elements: resistance, insurrection and constituent power. It is important to recognize, however, that, like the dominant concept of democracy, the dominant concept of counterpower was defined in modernity by the national space and by national sovereignty. The effect was that, during the modern era – at least since the French Revolution and throughout the long phase of socialist and communist agitation – the three elements of the concept of counterpower (resistance, insurrection and constituent power) tended to be viewed as external to one another, and thus functioned as different strategies, or at least different historical moments of revolutionary strategy. Once the elements were thus divided, the entire concept of counterpower tended to be reduced to one of its elements: the concept of insurrection or, really, civil war. Lenin's political thought is exemplary in this regard. For Lenin, counterpower – that is, in his terms, the dualism of power that consisted of the rise of a proletarian power against the bourgeoisie – could only exist for a very brief period, precisely for the period of insurrection. Resistance, which for Lenin principally took the form of syndicalist wage struggles, had an important political role but it was fundamentally separate from the revolutionary process. Constituent power, too, tended to disappear in Lenin's vision because every advance of constituent power immediately became an element of the new state, that is, transformed into a new constituted power. What remained of the revolutionary concept of counterpower was thus, for Lenin, primarily the great force of insurrection or, really, civil war against the dictatorship of the bourgeoisie.

Once we understand that the modern notion of counterpower reduces to insurrection, we should look more closely at the conditions and fortunes of modern insurrection. Paradoxically and tragically, even when the modern communist insurrection managed to win, it really lost, because it was immediately imprisoned in an alternation between national and international war. Finally, it becomes clear that national insurrection was really an illusion.

The Parisian Communards set the model in 1871 for all modern communist insurrection. Their example taught that the winning strategy was to transform international war into civil war – national, interclass war. International war was the condition of possibility for launching insurrection. The Prussians at the gates of Paris not only toppled the Second Empire of Louis Bonaparte, but also made possible the overthrow of Thiers and of the Republic. Paris armed is the revolution armed! Forty years later the Bolsheviks, too, needed the inter-European war, that is, the First World War, as the condition of insurrection. And once again the Germans, the national enemy, acted as condition of possibility. The Bolsheviks, too, transformed international war into civil war.

The tragedy of modern insurrection, however, is that national civil war is immediately and ineluctably transformed back into international war – or, really, into a defensive war against the united international bourgeoisie. A properly national, civil war is really not possible insofar as a national victory only gives rise to a new and permanent international war. Therefore, exactly the same condition that makes possible the national communist insurrection – that is, international war – is what imprisons the victorious insurrection or, rather, distorts it into a permanent military regime. The Parisian Communards were caught in this double bind. Marx saw clearly the mistakes of the Commune but did not show that the other options open to them would have equally been mistakes. The choice was between either giving all power to the Central Committee and marching on the bourgeois army at Versailles – that is, becoming a military regime – and being defeated and massacred. The process would not have ended with a victory at Versailles, either. The Prussian and the English ruling classes would not have allowed that. The victory of the Commune would have been the beginning of an unending international war. The Soviet victory only confirmed that double bind. The military victory in Russia, the complete defeat of the national bourgeoisie, only opened an international war (hot and then cold) that lasted for over seventy years.

Insurrection during the Cold War operated under the same structure, but only refined the model, reducing international war to its essential form. The Cold War fixed the conditions of modern insurrection into a permanent state. On the one hand, there was a permanent state of international war that was already coded in class terms. The representational structure of the two opposing powers forced its coding on all the new movements. The alternative was also decisive in material terms, since an insurrectionary movement could solicit the aid of one of the superpowers or play them off against one another. The formula for national insurrection was ready-made. But also ready-made and ineluctable were the limits of national insurrection. No movement could escape the great Cold War alternative. Even insurrectionary movements that did not conceive of themselves primarily in class terms – anti-colonial movements in Asia and Africa, anti-dictatorial movements in Latin America, black power movements in the US – were inevitably forced to be represented on one side of the great struggle. National insurrection during the Cold War was ultimately illusory. The victorious insurrection and the revolutionary nation were finally only pawns in the great Cold War chess game.

The contemporary relevance that emerges from this brief history of modern insurrection centres around two facts or, really, one fact with two faces. On the one hand, with the decline of national sovereignty today and the passage to Empire, gone are the conditions which allowed for the modern insurrection to be thought and, at times, to be practised. Today it thus seems almost impossible even to think insurrection. On the other hand, also gone is precisely the condition that kept modern insurrection imprisoned in the interminable play between national and international wars. Today, therefore, when considering the question of insurrection, we are faced both with a great difficulty and with an enormous possibility. Let us move back, however, to the more general consideration of counterpower.

A counterpower of monstrous flesh

With the contemporary decline of the sovereignty of the nation-state, it is possible once again to explore the concept of counterpower in its full form and return to its conceptual foundation.

Today the relationship betwen resistance, insurrection and constituent power has the possibility to be absolutely continuous, and in each of these moments it is possible to express the power of invention. In other words, each of the three moments – resistance, insurrection and constituent power – can be internal to one another, forming a common means of political expression. The context in which – and against which – this counterpower acts is no longer the limited sovereignty of the nation-state but the unlimited sovereignty of Empire, and thus counterpower, too, must be re-conceived in an unlimited or unbounded way.

Here we are faced with a new, imposing and exciting, theoretical and political problematic. In our present imperial context we need to rethink the concepts of resistance, insurrection and constituent power – and rethink, too, their internal connections, that is, their unity in the concept and practice of counterpower. When we look across the field of contemporary theoretical production we can see that we do already have some tools to work with on this terrain. Certainly, Michel Foucault's development of the concept of resistance, along with all the work that has emerged from his own – James Scott's notion of the 'weapons of the weak' and all the other studies on micropolitical resistance – should be a foundation for any investigation into this problematic. The great limitation of all this work, however, is that it never manages to discover the internal connection that resistance can have with insurrection and constituent power. In other words, resistance can be a powerful political weapon; but isolated individual acts of resistance can never succeed in transforming the structures of power.[6] Today, however, the other two components of counterpower remain completely undeveloped. An insurrection is a collective gesture of revolt, but what are the terms for insurrection today and how can it be put into practice? It should be clear that we can no longer translate insurrection immediately into civil war, as was so common in the modern era, if by 'civil' we mean a war within the national space. Insurrection is indeed still a war of the dominated against the rulers within a single society, but that society now tends to be an unlimited global society, imperial society as a whole. How is such an insurrection against Empire to be put into practice? Who can enact it? Where is the internal connection between the micropolitics of resistance and imperial insurrection? And how can we today conceive of constituent power, that is, of the common invention of a new social and political constitution? Finally, we need to think resistance, insurrection, and constituent power as one indivisible process, the three being forged together into a full counterpower and, ultimately, into a new alternative social formation. These are enormous questions and we are only at the very first stages of addressing them.

Rather than confronting them directly, it seems better to us to shift registers and take a different view on the entire

---

[6] From our perspective, Félix Guattari, especially in his work with Gilles Deleuze, is the one who has gone furthest to push the notion of resistance towards a conception of molecular revolution.

problematic. We have to find some way to shake off the shackles of reasonableness, to break out of the common forms of thinking about democracy and society, to create more imaginative and inventive perspectives. Let us begin by looking at the most basic foundation of counterpower, where its three elements – resistance, insurrection and constituent power – most intimately correspond. The primary material of counterpower is the flesh, the common living substance in which the corporeal and the intellectual coincide and are indistinguishable. Maurice Merleau-Ponty writes about the fact that flesh is neither matter, mind nor substance. Rather we should use the old term 'element' to act as a sort of incarnate principle or 'element' of Being (see this volume, p. 118).[7] The flesh is pure potentiality, the unformed stuff of life, an element of being. One should be careful, however, not to confuse the flesh with some notion of bare life, that is to say, one which conceives of a form of life stripped of all its qualities, a negative limit of life.[8] The flesh is oriented in the other direction, towards the fullness of life. We do not remain flesh; flesh is but an element of being; we continually make of our flesh a form of life.

In the development of forms of life, we discover ourselves as a multitude of bodies and at the same time we recognize that every body is itself a multitude – of molecules, desires, forms of life, inventions. Within each of us resides a legion of demons or, perhaps, of angels – this is the basic foundation, the degree zero of the multitude. What acts on the flesh and gives it form are the powers of invention, those powers that work through singularities to weave together hybridizations of space and metamorphoses of nature – the powers, in short, that modify the modes and forms of existence.

[7] Maurice Merleau-Ponty, *The Visible and the Invisible*, ed. Claude Lefort, trans. Alphonso Lingis (Northwestern University Press, Evanston, 1968), p. 139. Consider also Antonin Artaud's conception of the flesh: 'There are intellectual cries, cries born of the *subtlety* of the marrow. That is what I mean by Flesh. I do not separate my thought from my life. With each vibration of my tongue I retrace all the pathways of my thought in my flesh.' ('Situation of the flesh', in *Selected Writings*, ed. Susan Sontag, trans. Helen Weaver, University of California Press, Berkeley, 1988, p. 110)

[8] See Giorgio Agamben, *Homo Sacer: Sovereign Power and Bare Life*, trans. Daniel Heller-Roazen (Stanford University Press, Stanford, 1998).

In this context it is clear that the three elements of counterpower (resistance, insurrection and constituent power) spring forth *together* from every singularity and from every movement of bodies that constitute the multitude. Acts of resistance, collective gestures of revolt, and the common invention of a new social and political constitution pass together through innumerable micropolitical circuits – and thus in the flesh of the multitude is inscribed a new power, a counterpower, a living thing that is against Empire. Here are born the new barbarians, monsters and beautiful giants that continually emerge from *within* the interstices of imperial power and *against* imperial power itself. The power of invention is monstrous because it is excessive. Every true act of invention, every act, that is, which does not simply reproduce the norm is monstrous. Counterpower is an excessive, overflowing force, and one day it will be unlimited and unmeasurable. This tension between the excess and the unlimited is where the monstrous characteristics of the flesh and counterpower take on a heightened importance. As we are waiting for a full epiphany of the (resistant, revolting and constituent) monsters, there grows a recognition that the imperial system, that is, the contemporary form of repression of the will to power of the multitude, is at this point on the ropes, at the margins, precarious, continually plagued by crisis. (Here is where the weak philosophies of the margin, difference, and nakedness appear as the mystifying figures and the unhappy consciousness of imperial hegemony.)

Against this, the power of invention (or, really, counterpower) makes common bodies out of the flesh. These bodies share nothing with the huge animals that Hobbes and the other theorists of the modern state imagined when they made of the Leviathan the sacred instrument, the pitbull of the appropriative bourgeoisie. The multitude we are dealing with today is, instead, a multiplicity of bodies, each of which is criss-crossed by intellectual and material powers of reason and affect; they are cyborg bodies that move freely, without regard to the old boundaries that separated the human from the machinic. These multiple bodies of the multitude enact a continuous invention of new forms of life, new languages, new intellectual and ethical powers. The bodies of the multitude are monstrous, irrecuperable to the capitalist logic that tries continually to control it in the organization of Empire. The bodies of the multitude, finally, are queer bodies, unsusceptible to the forces of discipline and normalization but sensitive only to their own powers of invention. When we point to the powers of invention as a key to the formation of counterpower in the age of Empire, we do not mean to refer to some exclusive population of artists or philosophers. In the political economy of Empire, the power of invention has become the general and common condition of production. This is what we mean when we claim that immaterial labour and general intellect have come to occupy a dominant position in the capitalist economy.

If, as we have argued, the dominant form of democracy that modernity and European history has bequeathed us – popular, representational democracy – is not only unrealized but actually unrealizable, then one should not view our proposition of an alternative democracy of the multitude as a utopian dream. The unrealizability of the old notion of democracy should, rather, force us to move forward. This also means that we are entirely within and completely against imperial domination, and there is no dialectical path possible. The only invention that now remains for us is the invention of a new democracy, an absolute democracy, without boundaries and without measure. A democracy of powerful multitudes, not only of equal individuals but of powers equally open to cooperation, to communication, to creation. Here there are no programmes to propose – and who would still dare to do such a thing today, after the twentieth century has ended? All the modern protagonists – the priests, the journalists, the preachers, the politicians – may still be of use to imperial power, but not to us. The philosophical and artistic elements in all of us, the practices of working on the flesh and of dealing with its irreducible multiplicities, the powers of unlimited invention – these are the leading characteristics of the multitude. Beyond our unrealized democracy, there is a desire for a common life that needs to be realized. We can perhaps, mingling together the flesh and the intellect of the multitude, generate a new youth of humanity through an enormous enterprise of love.

7

LESSON 3

Political Subjects: On the Multitude and Constituent Power

In this lesson I shall deal first with the methodological under-pinnings of the definition of the concept of multitude, and then with the concept of *constituent power*.

As we know, the concept of multitude emerges in its most significant formulation in the work of Spinoza, who uses the term to mean a multiplicity of singularities which are placed in some kind of order. This is not to say that the concept of multitude was absent from the political thinking of modernity prior to Spinoza, but insofar as it was present it was with negative connotations. The concept of multitude referred essentially to the lack of order in a multiplicity of subjects, the multitude being seen as matter to be formed, rather than as material containing within itself a formative principle. Viewed in the light of Aristotelian categories, the multitude included no formal principle, no efficient principle and no final principle; it was simply a multiple, material body, on which one had to act, forming it from the outside. *In Spinoza, on the other hand, the concept of multitude takes on meaning precisely to the extent to which it lacks an idea of external causation.* Being rigidly immanentist and materialist, Spinoza denies the possibility of any cause external to reality. There is no God who establishes causal principles; there is no creation on the part of an external ordering power; nor is there any configuration of a finality; or, rather, matter is divine and creation is a process internal to matter.

Thus when Spinoza raises the problem of the organization of multiplicity and the problem of democracy, he approaches them in terms of immanence. In other words he asks himself how the multitude can organize itself directly (or, rather, how it organizes itself currently). From this point of view, the multitude is a concept which expresses *in and by itself* everything which previously it did not have: the cause becomes an act, a process, and *democracy* is the form through which the multitude (through the interaction of singularities) expresses common will. And this common will has no *outside*; it is entirely autonomous, and thus we shall call it absolute will. With Spinoza we are in the second half of the seventeenth century, in the period when absolute monarchy is at its height. This absoluteness of the multitude (as also that of democracy), which emerges in the thinking of Spinoza, is a truly subversive concept – the first time in modernity (after Machiavelli) that it is so strongly expressed. A subversive concept which in some senses relates to theories of the state and democracy as they were developed in the Protestant sects, particularly the most radical and revolutionary of them, where the sense of the divinity was tied to a new affirmation of the subject, and where the multitude was thus understood as an ensemble of subjectivities turned towards God, to the realization of his inscrutable command: in short, a multitude of singularities which seeks, and thus produces, transcendent values. In other respects there is in Spinoza, within this definition of the multitude allied to the thinking of the Protestant sects, the tradition of republican thought which was widespread in the seventeenth century. *The idea of the multitude and the idea of absolute democracy become one single project in republican thinking.* As is known and as I have already observed, republican thinking emerges out of the Italian Renaissance. In particular, it emerges from the critical understanding of the crisis of the Florentine republic that we find in Machiavelli. In his *Discorsi sopra la prima deca di Tito Livio* [*Discourses on the First Ten Books of Titus Livius*], Machiavelli describes Florentine democracy as being based on the movements of the proletarian classes (the people), who organize themselves in order to regain their freedom (the Republic) and in order to organize work in the city. In Machiavelli there is an enormous advance (compared to the theories elaborated in the previous centuries) in the analysis and theorization of the relationship between freedom and the economic preconditions (labour, its organization and so on) of freedom, between freedom and the civic preconditions of development, between freedom and forms of government. Now, Spinoza refers to Machiavelli directly when he goes on to develop *the* dispositif *of the multitude as absolute democracy.* To conclude: Machiavellianism comes down to us as a theory which is deeply democratic; it finds its terrain of application and development in the Protestant sects, and then goes on to feed the revolutionary movements in Central Europe and England, until eventually it crosses the Atlantic and plays its part in the founding of the American Constitution. This has been thoroughly documented in Pocock. What interests me is to stress the centrality of Spinoza in this development.

In Spinoza there is an additional element which is extremely important; an element which, reaching us across Nietzsche's contribution to contemporary thought, expresses itself in our own times in the philosophies of Deleuze and Foucault. I refer to the definition of *subjectivity* – political subjectivity as well as the concept of subjectivity *tout court* – *as a product of an ensemble of relations.* Thus, in defining the subject, it is no longer possible to base the definition on metaphysical elements: in particular, any element of self-consciousness is secondary, compared to the work of the multitude and to the product of the relations between singularities. Certainly singularities maintain their own force, but they maintain it within a relational dynamics, which makes it possible to construct, at the same time, itself and the whole of everything.

So in this way the subject comes to be defined through its relation to the whole, which means (to repeat ourselves) that the subject has no existence except in relationship, and that the juridical and political qualifications can be applied to it only through the play of interaction. For instance, the concept of property is subordinated to the relation between singularities: we do not find appropriative individualism in the republican current in the thinking of modernity. When we look at the history of political thought, it is in fact Hobbes who places possessive individualism at the centre of the constituent process of modernity. Hobbes sees individuals as being egotistical and appropriative. They are driven into relations with others not through love, but through fear and self-interest: individuals are continuously engaged in trying to resolve conflict in nature, necessary war, in their own favour. Things continue in that fashion until an agreement or contract is established: only a contract can establish peace and provide a way out of the state of war. This contract has two elements. The first step consists in a transfer, or rather an alienation, of the power of individuals to a power that is transcendent and sovereign. The second step involves the defining of the powers of the central sovereign authority: its job is to guarantee the peace and security of individuals and property. In Hobbes we find a sophisticated interest both in sovereign power, as a product of the alienation of the natural rights of individuals, and in the structure and guarantees of property. In Hobbes's thinking there is also an invocation of theology and of the presence of God (the Hobbesian system, which is very materialist, would not in itself require it) in order to guarantee, or rather absolutely overdetermine, the transfer of rights to the monarchy. Absolute monarchy is thus defined as God on earth, in other words as an absolute will which falls outside of any limits. Absolute, in this case, means precisely that only authority is free and unconstrained by limits.

But, at this point, what happens to individuals? Individuals, at the moment in which they alienate power, become a *people*, in other words they become the ensemble of the bearers of rights recognized by the monarch. Thus *the concept of the people appears in modernity as a production of the state* – 'people' understood as the ensemble of property-owning citizens (property is the fundamental *right*) who have abdicated their freedom in return for a guarantee of their property. Their freedom, having previously been an absolute natural right, now becomes a public (subjective) right. In other words it is the state that guarantees the degree and extent of individual freedom which is useful and appropriate to the operation of the state machine and to the reproduction of property relationships. Subjective rights are recognized only to the extent that they are fixed in juridical ordinance. This concept of state, people and rights has lasted through to the present day, as has the idea of sovereignty. In the traditional modern conception, the idea of 'people' preserves the two Hobbesian characteristics: first, that of a transfer of sovereignty; secondly, that of the composition of the people as an ensemble of property-owning individuals.

But, *to return to the concept of multitude* – in the last phase of modernity we often come upon other definitions of the multitude, definitions that nearly always derive from the impossibility of formalizing the multitude within the concept of people. With the development of capitalism and the emergence of a complex society strongly articulated into classes, what we begin to see is the idea of *the multitude as mass*. In this case the multitude is described as an ensemble which is massified, confused and indistinct, but nevertheless with a striking-power and/or a power of resistance. Manifestly the concept of mass thus defined presents some characteristic elements of the multitude, subjected to capitalist development in the production-forms of heavy industry; however, it is also true that this concept of mass lends itself badly to being conjugated with the development of the organization of labour, or rather of labour power, as realized during that same period. In fact, it is when the concept of multitude confronts the new forms in the organization of labour and society – that is, when it is analysed as a form of technical and political class composition – it is only then that it is possible to reconstruct the concept of multitude, no longer simply in political terms (as happened in the republican currents from the sixteenth to the eighteenth century), but in fact as a material and ontological indicator of a new phase in the development of capitalism, of society and – which is more important – of subjectivity.

In the postmodern phase, the concept of multitude relates to the existence of singularities defined by their capacity for expressing immaterial labour and by the *potenza* of reappropriating production through immaterial labour (through activity). We can say that *postmodern labour power exists in the form of the multitude* (and that, consequently, the political form of postmodern production is that of absolute democracy). This philosophical–political discussion of the present-day determinations of labour and of the production of subjectivity that derives from them brings us back to the concept of the 'social individual' presented and developed by Marx in the *Grundrisse*. For Marx, the social individual is a complex subject who is constituted in cooperation. However, this position is *too economistic* – in other words the subject is presented in Marx as an element which is essentially (perhaps exclusively) productive. But the idea of the multitude, as we have tried to reconstruct it, has (without taking away anything from the productive dimension) the huge advantage of showing the *potenza* of singularities to express themselves in all directions, to show themselves as a proliferation of freedom.

To summarize and conceptualize: when we speak of the multitude we are basically arguing three things. From a viewpoint of the sociology and philosophy of society, we see the multitude, above all, *as an ensemble*, as a multiplicity of *subjectivities*, or rather of *singularities*; secondly, we speak of the multitude as a *non-*working-class social class (here we have in mind the experience of the transformation of work in the transition from Fordism to post-Fordism, from the hegemony of material labour to that of immaterial labour); third and finally, in speaking of the multitude we refer to a *multiplicity* which is not reduced to that of mass, but which is *capable of autonomous*, independent, intellectual *development*; development of the potentialities (*potenze*) of labour, which enables labour power to put an end to the dialectics between servitude and sovereignty through the reappropriation of the instruments of labour and the mechanisms of cooperation. Working within this perspective and translating things into political terms, we can now introduce the hypothesis of *the multitude as democratic* potenza, since it is a conjoining of both freedom and labour, combining them in the production of the 'common'. It is clear that, if we speak in these terms, we erase any distinction between the political and the social, between productivity and the ethics of life. The multitude thus defined presents itself as a concept which is open, dynamic and constitutive. We are in the biopolitical. Here the concept of multitude begins to live entirely within the biopolitical.

The transition from categories of production to political categories, as far as the definition of the concept of multitude is concerned, is thus tightly correlated with the historical process. In my view, we should be very careful not to read the concept of multitude as unrelated to the categories of production which are organized around immaterial labour; but at the same time we have to see the transition from material labour to immaterial labour (a transition that gives substance to the construction of general intellect) as a transition which is historically determined. In the discussions which have been developing around the topics dealt with here, particularly regarding the interpretation of general intellect in linguistic terms, there is often a tendency to see general intellect as a result of *invariant* elements of production. What happens here is that a series of theoretical elements is absorbed into the methodology of workerism which draws on Chomsky's analysis of linguistic structure. But a discourse on linguistic invariants *à la* Chomsky is in direct contrast with the historical interpretation of the becoming and assertion of general intellect. At any rate, I believe that Foucauldian method has the upper hand here; I do not think that we can permit our methodology to restrict itself to generative structures that are fixed. *Naturalism cannot satisfy the transformative dynamics the class struggle brings about.* When linguistic characteristics are attributed to the concept of general intellect, the analysis has to develop not towards the search for linguistic invariants but to biopolitical determinations of general intellect itself. It has to give flesh and blood to general intellect, if we want it to extend into the concept of multitude. Those same linguistic characteristics have to find a powerful human character – drop the smooth and the peaceful in order to grasp the dense and the combative; language is a striation of being, and, like every striation, it is an ensemble of singularities. *Invariance thus has to be related back to the* potenza *of themultitude.*

The discussion developed thus far now allows us to deepen some theoretical consequences and other relevant concepts which have not been touched on in the course of this exposition.

For instance, at this point we need to clarify what we mean by *the concept of 'the common'* (and the whole family of related terms), as it has emerged from the definition of the multitude. In particular, we have to go beyond some traditional readings of the concept of the common, which relate it to identity and/or consensus. Here, obviously, we are dealing with concepts which, through the common and in the definition of the common, are often tied up with the concept of multitude. Let us start by saying that the multitude is neither a re-finding of identity, nor purely the exaltation of differences, but rather the acknowledgement that, behind identity and differences, there can exist a 'common-ness', or 'a common', whether it is understood as a *proliferation of creative activities* or as a diversity of relations and associative forms. The adoption of this image of the political subject is a decisively new political development compared with traditional political theories. The multitude is in fact an *ensemble* of singularities, wherein by 'ensemble' we mean a common-ness of differences, and where singularities are conceived of as the product of difference. The 'common' (in the multitude) is never the identical – it is not 'community' (*Gemeinschaft*): it is also not, purely, society (*Gesellschaft*), in other words a diversity of possessive individuals. If we move now from this ontological definition straight to the political, let us note immediately that it is no accident that people are talking today about the 'movement of movements' as a new configuration of organizational processes of democratic subjects, capable of expressing political *potenza*. In this area, then, we shall have to criticize and go beyond the traditional concept of *consensus*. Consensus is a name and an idea tied to those of people and representation: consensus is adherence and alienation, identification with the representative. It is no accident that the concept of consensus has come to be increasingly identified with that of *consumption*. This approach to consensus raises the problem of a new definition, involving a going beyond *representation*. Whereas representation is a concept involving the *alienation* of the potencies of the citizens in favour of the modern monarch, and consensus is *a metaphor* of this process, the problem that we face is quite another: how to give political form to *the expression of the multitude* within this process, a political form which is not one of alienation of the productive *potenza* and of freedom of the subjects. This is very much an open question, and it means that we have to elaborate new ideas, and in particular analyse the *mechanisms of cooperation which are formed within, and extended via, the networks*. Do forms of productive cooperation exist, in terms of freedom (and hence a cooperation which has no boss and does not have the necessity of transferring the ability to produce onto some capacity for command)?

Later we shall see that, in the functioning of language, we have not only the possibility of being equal in expressing meaning, but also the possibility of recognizing that meaning is born from, is formed within, linguistic cooperation. In this perspective we can identify the interlinking of the revolution in production and the linguistic revolution, the determination of the ontological–productive transformation under way, where productive value and linguistic meaning construct a common trajectory.

Moving ahead on these issues, it would be useful to deepen our analysis of the concept of multitude. It was developed by writers in the area of *postmodern philosophy*, pursuing various different points of view: we need to take a position in relation to this diversity. The theorists of postmodernity give a definition of the subject which sees it as a 'weak subject', one which is evanescent. The project of Lyotard, Baudrillard, Rorty and other European and American philosophers has been to define the subject as a figure without a preconstituted, preconceived and ontologically grounded identity. This has all occurred not only within philosophy; also has powerful applications in the theory of justice. For example, in Rawls we find an affirmation of the subject which is in line with what is expressed in postmodern philosophical thought. The subject, says Rawls, lives in the shadow, and it is only by raising the surrounding veils that the subject can learn to constitute community. In short, it seems that Rawls, in agreement with the postmodernists, wants to show the impossibility of the subject producing togetherness, cooperation and the common: if he does not succeed in this, it will then be necessary to take the analysis of subjectivity back to the Hobbesian premise. And, since the subject does not in fact succeed in this, it is only external power, the power of the state, of capital, that can create the ensemble: but in a weak way. There is no war, but there is ignorance, and it continues to operate in a veil of obscurity. Other positions apart from that of Rawls have approached the postmodern political theme in similar terms. For example we have Rorty's position, which states strongly that subjectivation can no longer be given in classic bourgeois (and thus constructive) terms, in other words taking as its starting point the hypothesis of bourgeois civil war and the independence of individuals.

But there is also another tendency within this philosophical-political perception, namely the writers who reintroduce a *communitarian*-type narrative. The most obvious example in Anglo-Saxon philosophy is Michael Sandel. In his thinking, and in the schools associated with him, the subject is presented as a weak subject, and it is only to the extent that it is determined by the state that it becomes strong. What we have here is an attempt to construct intermediate forms capable of mediating the weak relationships of civil society. Examining these left-wing developments of weak thought for what they say about subjectivity, we note the failure of the project of establishing an institutional (legal and normative) convergence between subjectivity and the constitution of the common. This failure becomes increasingly apparent as the attempt is no longer pursued at the institutional level of the nation-state, but at international level. Indeed this school of thought claims to be able to imagine, on the international scene, a kind of 'civil society' acting as mediator between the interests of states and global commonness . . . (The results of such attempts have often been disastrous.)

That said, it is clear that the problem is one of understanding how we define the multitude as a *strong* concept rather than a weak one. Resolving this problem means setting up a distinction between *limit* and *obstacle*, and then moving forward on that terrain. So, one has a limit when the blockage imposed on activity is such that it is no longer possible to do activity of any kind. Limit is something totally negative. Obstacle, on the other hand, is when there is something outside or ahead of us preventing us from moving forward or acting differently. Limit is an ontological determination, something indestructible. Stressing the definition of limit means understanding that the multitude is something that sovereignty and power can no longer destroy and which, come what may, they are obliged to endure and eventually mediate. Now let us turn to the definition of obstacle. Working on the notion of obstacle will mean understanding how the multitude (understood negatively as the limit of sovereignty) presents itself positively as an ensemble of singularities, of class and of *potenza*, which is always in relation to an obstacle. How will the multitude deal with the obstacle? In the history of political thought there are different positions around this problem. *In the traditional conception of communism*, but also already in radical democratic theories, for instance in Jacobinism and the like, the obstacle is presented as something which must be destroyed. The obstacle is always too strong to be got around. There is here a single overturning: rather than feeling itself, as such, to be the insuperable limit of sovereignty, the multitude is here conceived only as obstacle and becomes devalued and underrated; consequently, the multitude thinks that it can express itself only through the destruction of the monarch. In this case it over-values the monarch, the enemy. Its problem will be that of liberating itself from the state, and of establishing the dictatorship of the proletariat. This is a small way out, because the dictatorship of the proletariat is still an image, albeit reversed, of state. *Our position is the opposite:* the problem is how to ensure the prevailing of the force of the multitude as an indestructible power. It has no need of dictatorship (and thus has no need for the action and legitimacy of an overthrown state) in order to set the revolutionary process in motion. The problem of liberation from labour, from bosses, from the capitalist, is put in the same way and in the same relations. The obstacle is there ahead – *whereas the multitude is a limit for the state, the state is only an obstacle for the multitude.* All this requires that there should be a striking force capable of developing and/or maintaining the confrontation, capable of making decisions about force: one example from this point of view is the Leninist conception of the party (which we must again take up as a problematic index, as a highlighting of the ontological function of the limit, of which the multitude is the bearer). Let us now complicate the argument and ask the following: in radical democratic theories the relationship, or the clash, between the multitude and obstacle requires, in fact demands, a place, a location, in which this can take place; but when the multitude presents itself as an ensemble of productive and proliferating singularities, then the actual location of the confrontation itself becomes problematic. Or, rather, there is no longer any single place of confrontation – the confrontation is everywhere. If we now tie all this in to our general methodology, we recall that *Empire also has no place.* And when we say that Empire has no place, we also say that the multitude has no place. In other words we are in a situation where the multitude is diffused everywhere. *Empire and the multitude have mechanisms of formation that are in some sense analogous despite their absolute difference and their absolute opposition.* So, now, how do we find a way to deal with the question of obstacle within this framework?

In order to construct a theory of the smashing of the obstacle we need first to return to some of the statements that have emerged in the course of our discussion. The first relates to the analysis of immaterial labour, the hegemony of which we have recognized within the social organization of labour. Now, *immaterial labour does not require command.* The diffusion of knowledge in networked forms thus offers itself, potentially, as being in excess of the obstacles that confront it. The multitude of immaterial labour thus lives through excess, through exodus. At this point a second definition is added to our statement regarding the *dispositif* (that is, the relation and/or concatenation) of immaterial labour and exodus. This definition relates to the fact that, today, *labour, in order to be creative, must be 'common', in other words produced by networks of cooperation.* Labour is defined ontologically as freedom through the common: labour is productive when it is free, otherwise it is dead, and it is free only when it is common. The problem of the obstacle, then, presents itself in these terms, as something that stands in the way of the common dimension. Getting over the obstacle therefore means giving life both to the common dimension and to the exodus from capitalism, together.

We can now arrive at some conclusions. First, we say that the *potenza* of the multitude can eliminate the sovereign relation, inasmuch as the multitude proposes itself as absolute limit. Analogously, we can say that while the production of the sovereign power may get over the obstacle, it is unable to eliminate the limit which the multitude poses. Secondly, it can be said that the production of the multitude is at the same time both being and limit. This last point requires additional clarification. We have said that sovereignty, as an eminent figure of the capitalist relation, is a relation between the person who commands and the person who obeys. Now the question is: where is the true limit of sovereignty to be found? *The limit of sovereignty lies in the relationship itself between the one who commands and the one who obeys.* The power of the multitude consists in the possibility not so much of destroying this relation, but of emptying it, of leaving it behind, of causing it to fail through a radical negation. *The multitude is the negation of the relationship.* It is the multitude, in fact, which produces and reproduces the world. It is precisely for this reason that the multitude constitutes the limit of the relation of sovereignty. This is the real possibility that we have for giving meaning to the concept of multitude, beyond the tradition and the alternatives of modern political science: a real and concrete experimentation, a very broad-ranging phenomenology at the level of labour, the political, property, appropriation, legal relationships with the rest of the world, in other words the basic areas of concern on any definition of politics.

There is beginning to be an extensive bibliography on the concept of multitude and the problems of its definition, but here a reference to two books will suffice: Paulo Virno, A Grammar of the Multitude: For an Analysis of Contemporary Forms of Life, *Semiotexte, Los Angeles, 2004; and Marco Bascetta, 'Moltitudine, popolo, massa', in the joint-authored volume* Controimpero. Per un lessico dei movimenti globali *[Counter-Empire: Towards a Lexicon of Global Movements],* Manifestolibri, Rome, 2002, pp. 67–80.

For the historical genesis of the concept of multitude the reader may find useful my Anomallia selvaggia *[The Savage Anomaly. The Power of Spinoza's Metaphysics and Politics,* University of Minnesota Press, Minneapolis, 1993]. *The book was published by Feltrinelli in 1981 and can now be found in an edition published by DeriveApprodi (Rome, 1998). In my work on Spinoza, apart from exploring the originality of his political philosophy, I try to reconstruct an alternative approach to the politics of the sovereign state which, in the modern era, extends from Machiavelli through Spinoza to Marx. The concept of multitude is thus developed within this historical context and constitutes an alternative tradition within modernity.*

For another text on the modern precursors of the concept of multitude, see Laurent Bove, La Stratégie du conatus. Affirmation et résistance chez Spinoza, *Vrin, Paris, 1996; and, lastly, the thesis by Filippo Del Lucchese (Ph.D. thesis, University of Pisa 2002; published Ghibli, 2004), 'Tumulti e* indignatio. Conflitto, diritto e moltitudine in Machiavelli e Spinoza' *(Tumults and* Indignatio: Conflict, Law and Multitude in Machiavelli and Spinoza).

For more on the concept of multitude, see also pp. 114–25 below, where the multitude is considered from three points of view: the multitude as a multiple ensemble of singularities; the multitude as a class concept (not simply working-class); and finally the multitude as an ontological potenza. *It is clear that, as is stressed throughout this book, these alternatives form, and act entirely within, the modifications of the paradigm of production (where production is understood in biopolitical terms).*

In what we have said so far in this lesson we have not yet addressed the question of constitution. *The multitude has presented itself to us as limit of sovereignty (and no longer simply as an obstacle to it): but the fact of being limit, and being a limit in biopolitical terms, means to be powerful* [potenti]. The multitude is *potenza*. The fact of its existence is constituent. *The multitude is entirely rooted in the new paradigm of production, but precisely for this reason the common that characterizes it as a precondition is in itself productive and constituent. For myself, I have written extensively on the constituent multitude in* Il potere costituente. Saggio sulle alternative del moderno, *second expanded edition, Manifestolibri, Rome 2001* [Insurgencies: Constituent Power and the Modern State, *University of Minnesota Press, Minneapolis, 1999]; a series of positions regarding the constituent multitude can also be found in M. Hardt and A. Negri,* Il lavoro di Dionisio. Per la critica dello Stato postmoderno), *second edition, Manifestolibri, Rome 2001* [Labor of Dionysus. A Critique of the State Form, *University of Minnesota Press, Minneapolis, 1994]. For a more philosophical reading (on the constituent concept of the multitude and its precursors), see* Thousand Plateaus *by G. Deleuze and F. Guattari* [University of Minnesota Press, Minneapolis, 1987], *as well as A. Negri,* Kairos, Alma Venus, Multitudo. Nove lezioni impartite a me stesso, *Manifestolibri, Rome 2000* [Kairos, Alma Venus, Multitudo, *in* Time For Revolution, *Continuum, London, 2003*].

The two latter texts provide a particularly useful basis for a critique of the approach of postmodern philosophies to the experience of the multitude. As we know, weak thought and negative thought, both indebted to soft versions of the thought of Nietzsche, have preferred to see the multitude as an ensemble of subjects fading away and becoming uncertain, rather than considering the common as a sign of a new constituent capability. Often the philosophies of postmodernity have come close to mystical/religious experience; particularly around the topic of the multitude (that is, of the new subjectivation and the new pluralism). When postmodernity is taken instead positively and the subjectivity of the multitude is reclaimed, then the grand narrative once again becomes possible. Not that the subjects present themselves as metaphysical entities and/or entities preconstituted in a teleological process: quite the contrary, the *telos* of the common is something that is constructed, constituted, step by step; *it is the untimely character of an imaginary which precariously, but nonetheless effectively, is being constituted.* Constituent power is defined here: where the multitude seeks to construct itself anew through subjectivity, and the virtual thus presents itself as more real than the real. Constituent power is not something that is prefigured but comes to be formed in untimely and aleatory form, yet is none the less effective. It is the efficacy of the struggle, of the claims of the multitude, of the *potenza* of its movements – this is what invents and constitutes new reality. The political is the basic stage-setting in this process. *Thus between the multitude and constituent power there exists an unbreakable bond.* It happens that I set out to theorize constituent power before fully theorizing the concept of multitude: this was a mistake. As my research advanced, trans-posing itself ever more clearly from the political historical level to the political–institutional level, the relation was inverted and the multitude preceded constituent power. In modern history con-stituent power is a moment of invention in history-in-the-making; always, in the political thinking of modernity, constituent power is viewed as a sudden emergence, and can be defined precisely only within this perspective of immediacy. Lenin himself, who wrote in *State and Revolution* some of the finest pages we have on constituent power, sees it as a power that cannot last for long . . . *the concept of multitude, however, gives to constituent power a completely different dimension; in a sense, it modifies its time and space.* If in fact the multitude is an ensemble of acting singularities, constituent *potenza* cannot be anything other than the action of the common *telos* of the multitude. Constituent power is the organizational dynamic of the multitude, its becoming. In the following lessons we shall go into this process more deeply, never forgetting that the multitude is not only constituent of political orders but (on the biopolitical stage), but also constitutive of being.

Here we need to stress once again that *potenza* cannot be reduced to *potere*, just as the many cannot be reduced to the one. There is no dialectics between *potenza* and *potere*, nor is there a dialectics between the many and the one. Our logic (like that which in modernity is opposed to the statist reduction of the multitude) speaks of another *telos*, another formative *raison*, another way of constructing life. In each of these cases, the most important word is *other*: 'other' rather than 'against', because 'other' is singular, and 'against' can end up with reversed homologies, reintroducing us into the relation of sovereignty or that of capital. The notion of absolute singularities is, however, something quite other, relat-able to 'haecceity', as Deleuze has shown. Singularity and haecceity are graspable not in themselves but inasmuch as they express excedence. This is also the way Duns Scotus explains haecceity: here it is a concept of a specific and creative difference. It has no measure, and when it has *telos* it is a *telos* that has nothing to do with teleology, because it is not a preconstitution of the destiny of the world. Here we are on the terrain of an absolute freedom, and the *telos* is the product of an excedence, of an activity . . . It is a bit strange to be seeking in Duns Scotus the responsibility for a definition of haecceity, even if a long tradition allows us to do so. In fact the concept of singularity, in the way we use it in the definition of the multitude, is a post-structuralist concept. In other words it is the concept of a subject who participates in a whole without being a product of it, of a determination which participates in a class without being a function of that class, of a worker who produces a product which is not abstract (and thus in which his or her labour is alienated), but which is concretely expressive of his or her *potenza*. Therefore when we refer to the multitude as 'an ensemble of singularities', we are talking about different singularities, which are never identified in the whole; nor are they ever substantialized as separate individuals. *The singularity both is made by the whole and makes the whole.* In French post-structuralist thought, and in particular in Deleuze, the attempt to give a strong character to the singularity, while removing from it any substance, sometimes seems to result in indifferentiation. But this is simply how it appears. *What in fact sustains singularity, even when it presents itself without substance, is its constituent capacity, its potenza.* Constituent power, war machines, new subjectivities, all this qualifies and powerfully determines the production of common being. This, then, is the concept of singularity to which we refer. Here again, we are alluding to the Spinozian notion of *potenza*, which is as different from Aristotelian *potenza** as is a non-teleological cause from a cause which in every instance constructs finality and destiny; as different as desire (that great vital force that drives you up, from instinct to the love of God; this excedence that continually produces) is from naturalistic pre-determination. The materialism of the excedent cause and of the immanent *telos* is at the base of every process of production of subjectivity. Think of what has happened since Seattle and the

---

* [*Translator's note*: The reference here is to Aristotle's notion of *dynamis*, 'potentiality', which is rendered in Italian through *potenza*.]

movements around Genoa: this is how the singularity realizes in common a new imaginary and translates labour into activity.

General intellect: as we know, this concept already has a long history, being contained in Marx's *Grundrisse* (written in 1858–9 but only published in Russia by the Marx–Engels Institute in 1954). The first notable aspect of its history is the fact that general intellect, which was a late arrival within the already consolidated dogmatics of Marxist interpretation, inevitably ended up being mistreated within that debate – a debate in which the sound of quotations being fired off often gave way to actual gunfire . . . The *Grundrisse* had the good fortune to be published later. In the second issue of *Quaderni Rossi*, published in 1962, Solmi translated the 'Fragment on machines', in other words the fragment in which Marx speaks of general intellect as a fundamental pillar of production, and therefore of the overcoming of the law of value, and of the coming into being of the 'social individual' as the sole producer of wealth. From that point there emerged various interpretations, always heterodox, of general intellect. Although some people played up the 'prophetic power' of these pages with the intention of caricaturing them and eliminating them from a positive interpretation, a second reading was also offered: working-class subjectivity, grounded in immaterial labour and technical-scientific knowledge, traversed the era of the mass worker (in the triumph of Fordism) to propose itself as hegemonic in production. As early as 1968 we, workerists [*operaisti*] had already grasped this *potenza* of general intellect – namely in 1968, because at that time the student revolt opened the debate about intellectual labour power and capitalist reaction tried to turn the latter into the central moment of the reorganization of development. At this point a further debate emerged: general intellect was viewed no longer simply as a paradigm of the intellectualization of production, but as a symptom and symbol of its socialization. In this transition there were many interpretative ruptures: on the one hand, those who simply considered knowledge as a revolutionary force; on the other, those who saw intellectual labour power as a subversive force. This division was particularly strong in France and Germany, and in the USA. A further phase of discussion opened in the 1980s, particularly the late 1980s, when general intellect, already socialized, begins to be interpreted in subjective terms. From being a function of capitalism, general intellect thus begins to be seen as a *dispositif* which is directly subjective and revolutionary. There are, naturally, others who continue to define general intellect in objective terms, comparing its structure to that of language. This has been extremely important for creating understandings about the mode of production typical of general intellect (general intellect and the digital mode of production); but, as I said earlier, in this case (in other words when general intellect and language tend to merge) it is even more necessary to give flesh and blood to this synthesis.

8

Towards an Ontological Definition of the Multitude*

1 The multitude is the name of an *immanence*. The multitude is an ensemble of singularities. If we take these statements as our starting point, they give us the outline of an ontological definition of the *reality that remains* once the concept of 'people' has been freed from transcendence. We are familiar with the way in which, in the hegemonic tradition of modernity, the concept of people was created. Hobbes, Rousseau and Hegel, each one for his part and in different ways, produced the concept of 'people' moving from the starting point of sovereign transcendence: in the minds of those writers, the multitude was seen as chaos and war. The thought of modernity operates in a double manner on this base: on the one hand it extracts the multiplicity of singularities and unifies it in transcendental manner in the concept of people; on the other, it dissolves the ensemble of singularities (which constitute the multitude) into a mass of individuals. Modern natural law, whether empiricist in origin or idealist, is thought of in terms of transcendence and dissolution of the level of immanence. The theory of the multitude, on the other hand, requires that subjects speak on their own account, and that here we are not dealing with *property-owning individuals, but with non-representable singularities.*

* First published in *Multitudes*, No. 9, Paris, May–June 2002.

2   The multitude is a class concept. The multitude is, in fact, always productive and always in movement. When viewed from a synchronic–temporal point of view, the multitude is exploited in production; and when it is viewed from a diachronic–spatial point of view, the multitude is also exploited, inasmuch as it constitutes productive society, social cooperation for production.

The class concept of multitude must be considered differently from the concept of working class. The concept of working class is in fact a limited concept, both in terms of actual production (it comprises basically only industrial workers) and in terms of social cooperation (it represents only a fraction of the workers engaged in the overall system of social production). Rosa Luxemburg's polemic against the crude workerism of the Second International and against the theory of the working-class aristocracy was an anticipation of the name of the multitude; it was no accident that Luxemburg accompanied her polemic against the working-class aristocracies with a polemic against the nationalism that was emerging in the working-class movement of her time.

If we institute the multitude as a class concept, the notion of *exploitation* will be defined as exploitation *of cooperation*; here it is no longer a cooperation of *individuals* but of *singularities*, an exploitation of the ensemble of singularities, of the networks which compose the ensemble, of the ensemble which comprises the networks and so on.

Note that the 'modern' conception of exploitation (as described by Marx) is functional to a conception of production in which individuals are made the actors. It is only because there are individuals who carry out work that labour is measurable by the law of value. The concept of mass (as an indefinite multiple of individuals) is also a *concept of measure*, or rather it has been constructed in the political economy of labour for this purpose. In this sense the mass is the counterpart of capital, in the same way the people is the counterpart of sovereignty. We might add that, not coincidentally, the concept is – particularly in the Keynesian and welfarist refinement of political economy – a measure. The exploitation of the multitude, on the other hand, is incommensurable – in other words it is a power related to singularities outside of measure and to a cooperation beyond measure.

If one defines our historical transition as *epochal* (ontologically so), this means that the criteria and the mechanisms of *measure*, which were valid for an earlier era, have been brought radically into question. We are living through this transition, and it is not guaranteed that new centres or mechanisms of measure are being proposed.

3   The multitude is the concept of a *potenza*. Already in analysing cooperation, we find that the ensemble of singularities produces *beyond meaure*. This *potenza* not only seeks to expand itself, but above all it seeks to conquer a body: *the flesh of the multitude* seeks to transform itself into *the body of general intellect*.

When we analyse this transition, or rather this self-expression of *potenza*, we can track it along three lines:

(a)   The genealogy of the multitude in the transition *from modernity to postmodernity* (or, if you prefer, from Fordism to post-Fordism). This genealogy is constituted by class struggles which dissolved the forms of social discipline characteristic of 'modernity'.

(b)   The tendency towards general intellect. The tendency, constitutive of the multitude, towards modes of productive expression that are increasingly immaterial and intellectual seeks to configure itself as an absolute recuperation of general intellect within living labour.

(c)   The liberty and the joy (but also the crisis and the toil) of this innovative transition, which includes within itself continuities and discontinuities; in short, something that can be defined as systoles and diastoles in the recomposition of singularities.

Again, we have to stress that the concept of multitude is different from that of people. The multitude is no longer grasped or explained in terms of contractualism (I mean that contractualism, rather than deriving from an empirical experience, derives from transcendental philosophy). In the more general sense, the multitude does not trust representation, because it is an incommensurable multiplicity. The people is always represented as a unity, whereas *the multitude is not representable*, because it is monstrous in relation to the teleological and transcendental rationalisms of modernity. In contrast with the concept of people, the concept of multitude is a singular multiplicity, a concrete universal. The people constituted a social body; the multitude does not, because the multitude is the flesh of life. If on the one hand we mark a contrast between the multitude and the people, on the other we also have to contrast the multitude to the masses and the plebs. The masses and the plebs have often been used as terms to name an irrational and passive social force, seen as dangerous and violent precisely because it was easily manipulable. The multitude, on the other hand, is an active social actor, a multiplicity which acts. The multitude is not a unit, as the people is; but, in contrast to the masses and the plebs we can see it as *something organized*. In effect, it is an active actor of self-organization. This very great advantage of the concept of multitude is that it sweeps away all the modern arguments based on the 'fear of the masses', and also those related to the 'tyranny of the majority' – arguments which have often served as a kind of blackmail, to oblige us to accept (and often to request) our own servitude.

As far as power is concerned, what is to be done with the multitude? Effectively there really is nothing that power can do with it, because here the categories that interest power, in other words the unity of the subject (people), the form of its composition (contract between people) and the mode of government (monarchy, aristocracy and democracy, whether separately or combined) have been set aside. On the other hand, that radical modification of the mode of production which has come about through the hegemony of immaterial labour power and of cooperating living labour – a real and proper ontological, productive and biopolitical revolution – has overturned all the parameters of 'good government' and has destroyed the modernist idea of a community that should function for capitalist accumulation, precisely as the capitalists desired it from the start.

The concept of multitude thus introduces us into a completely new world, within a revolution that is taking place. We ourselves can only imagine ourselves as monsters within this revolution. Gargantua and Pantagruel, in the fifteenth and sixteenth centuries, in the middle of the revolution that constructed modernity, were giants who served as extreme emblematic figures of freedom and invention: they traverse the revolution and propose the gigantic undertaking of achieving freedom. Today we need new giants and new monsters, who can put together nature and history, work and politics, art and invention, to show the new power that the birth of general intellect, the hegemony of immaterial labour and the new abstract passions of the activity of the multitude attribute to humanity. We need a new Rabelais, or rather, many of them.

Thus the raw material of the multitude is *flesh*, or that *common* living substance in which the body and the intellect coincide and are indistinguishable. 'The flesh is not matter, is not mind, is not substance,' Maurice Merleau-Ponty writes. 'To designate it, we should need the old term "element", in the sense it was used to speak of water, air, earth, and fire, that is, in the sense of a *general thing* . . . a sort of incarnate principle that brings a style of being wherever there is a fragment of being. The flesh is in this sense an "element" of Being.' Like flesh, the multitude is thus pure potentiality, the non-formed force of life, an element of being. Like flesh, the multitude also is oriented towards the fullness of life. The revolutionary monster which is called multitude and which appears at the end of modernity seeks continually to transform our flesh into new forms of life.

We can explain the movement of the multitude from flesh to the new forms of life from another point of view. It is internal to the ontological transition, it constitutes it. I mean that the *potenza* of the multitude, *viewed from the singularities* that comprise it, can reveal the dynamics of its enrichment, consistence and liberty. The production of singularity is in fact (as well as, globally, the production of commodities and the reproduction of society) a singular production of new subjectivity. Today, furthermore (in the immaterial mode of production which characterizes our epoch), it is very difficult to distinguish the production of commodities and the social reproduction of subjectivity, since there is no such thing as new markets without new needs, nor is there production of life without singular desire. At this point I would be interested to stress the global *potenza* of the process: it extends between globality and singularity according to a first rhythm (synchronic) of connections that are more or less intense (they have been called 'rhizomatic') and another rhythm (diachronic) of systoles and diastoles, of evolution and crisis, of concentration and dissipation of the flow. In short, the production of subjectivity, or the production of itself which the subject enacts, is *at the same time* the production of consistency of the multitude – because the multitude is an ensemble of singularities. Of course, some people suggest that the multitude is (in large part) a concept which is impossible to advance, which it is metaphorical, because a unity of the multiple can only be given through a more or less dialectical transcendent act (of the kind philosophy has operated, from Plato to Hobbes to Hegel); all the more so, if the multitude (or the multiplicity which refuses to represent itself in the dialectical *Aufhebung*) claims itself to be also singular and subjective. But the objection is weak: here in fact the dialectical *Aufhebung* is ineffective, because the unity of the multiple is, for the multitude, the same as the living, and the living is very hard to subsume within the dialectic. Furthermore, that mechanism of the production of subjectivity which has a common figure in the multitude reveals itself to be a *collective praxis*, or an ever-renewed activity which is constitutive of being. *The name 'multitude' is, at one and the same time, both subject and product of collective praxis.*

It is clear that the origins of the discourse on multitude are to be found in the subversive interpretation of the thinking of Spinoza. I can never tire of stressing the importance of the Spinozan premise in the treatment of this thematic. And one highly Spinozist theme is that of the body, and particularly that of the potent body. 'You do not know of how much a body is capable.' Now, the multitude is the name of a multitude of bodies. Of this determination we spoke when we stressed 'the multitude as *potenza*'. The body is thus *first* in terms of both genealogy and tendency, both in the phases and in the result of the process of constitution of the multitude. But this is not enough. We have to reconsider the whole discussion pursued thus far from the point of view of the body, in other words return to points (1), (2) and (3) of the preceding treatment and to complete them in the terms of this perspective.

To 1   Where we define the name of the multitude against the concept of people, and where we recall that the multitude is an ensemble of singularities, we need to translate that name in terms of the body – in other words, to clarify the *dispositif* of a multitude of bodies. When we look at bodies, we realize that we are not only in the presence of a multitude of bodies, but we also understand that *every body is a multitude*. Crossing each other in the multitude, crossing the multitude with the multitude, bodies intermingle, become subject to *métissage*, become hybridized, transform themselves; they are like the waves of the sea, in perennial movement and in perennial reciprocal transformation. The metaphysics of individuality (and/or of the person) are a fearsome mystification of the multitude of bodies. *There is no possibility for a body of being alone.* One cannot even imagine it. When one defines the human being as an individual, when one considers this being as an autonomous source of rights and of properties, one renders this being solo. But one's self does not exist except in relation to the other. The metaphysics of individuality, when they deal with the body, deny the multitude that constitutes the body, to deny the multitude of the bodies. Transcendence is the key to every metaphysics of individuality, as it is to every metaphysics of sovereignty. From the point of view of the body, on the other hand, there is only relation and process. The body is living labour, and thus expression and cooperation, and thus material construction of the world and of history.

To 2   At the point where we spoke of the multitude as a class concept, and thus of the multitude as a subject of production and object of exploitation, at that point, therefore, it will be immediately possible to introduce the bodily dimension, since it is obvious that, in production and in movements, in work and in migration, it is bodies that are in play. In all their dimensions and vital determinations. In production the activity of bodies is always a force of production, and is often raw material. Furthermore, there is no possibility of a discourse on exploitation, whether related to the production of commodites or to the reproduction of life, that does not touch bodies directly. Now, the concept of capital (on the one hand, production of wealth, on the other, exploitation of the multitude) must always be viewed realistically too, through the analysis of how much bodies are made to suffer, are worn down or mutilated or wounded, and generally reduced to being material of production. Matter is the same as commodity. And, while one cannot think that bodies are simply commodified in the production and reproduction of capitalist society, one must also stress the reappropriation of goods and the satisfaction of desires – not to mention the metamorphoses and the potentialization of bodies, which the struggle against capital determines – yet, once this structural ambivalence has been recognized, within the historical process of accumulation, one then has to raise the problem of its *solution* in terms of a *liberation of bodies* and of a project to struggle to that end. In short, a materialist *dispositif* of the multitude can only move from the priority consideration of the body and of the struggle against its exploitation.

To 3   We spoke of the multitude as the name of a *potenza*, and thus of genealogy and tendency, of crisis and transformation; hence the discourse has to do with the *metamorphosis* of bodies. The multitude is a multitude of bodies, it expresses *potenza* not only as an ensemble but also as singularities. Each period of the history of human development (of labour and of power, of needs and of the desire for transformation) brings with it singular *metamorphoses* of bodies. Historical materialism, too, contains a law of evolution: but this law is anything but necessary, linear or unilateral; it is the law of discontinuity, of leaps, of unexpected syntheses. It is Darwinian in the good sense, as a product of a Heraclitan clash and of an aleatory teleology, from below. This is so because the cause of the metamorphoses, which invest the multitude as an ensemble and the singularities as the multitude, is nothing other than struggles, movements, and desires for transformation.

With this we do not want to deny that sovereign power is capable of producing history and subjectivity. But sovereign power is a double-faced power: the production of power can act within the relation, but not remove it. Rather, sovereign power (as a relation of forces) can find itself facing, as a problem, an extraneous power which sets an obstacle against it: this, the first time. A second time, sovereign power finds, in the very relation that constitutes it and in the necessity of maintaining it, *its* limit. The relation is thus presented to sovereignty the first time as *obstacle* (wherein sovereignty acts within the relation), and a second time as *limit* (where sovereignty wishes to remove the relation, but does not succeed). On the contrary, *the* potenza *of the* multitude (of the singularities which work, are active, and sometimes disobey: but at any rate exist) *can eliminate the sovereign relation.*

We thus have two propositions (the first is: 'the production of sovereign power can get round the obstacle, but it cannot eliminate the limit which is constituted by the relation of sovereignty'; the second is: 'on the other hand the power of the multitude can eliminate the sovereign relation, because only the production of the multitude constitutes being') which can sustain the opening to an *ontology of the multitude*. This ontology will begin to be revealed when the constitution of being which is attributed to the production of the multitude can be practically determined.

To us it appears possible, from a theoretical point of view, to develop the axiom of the ontological *potenza* of the multitude on at least three levels. The *first* is that of theories of work, where the relation of command can (on the terrrain of immanence) be shown to be non-existent: immaterial, intellectual labour, in short, knowledge, which requires command in order to become cooperative and thus to have universal effects. On the contrary: knowledge is always in excess over the (mercantile) values within which anyone might try to enclose it. In the *second* place, the demonstration can be given directly on the ontological terrain, or on that *experience of the common* (which does not require either command or exploitation) which institutes itself as the basis and premise of every human productive and/or reproductive expression. Language is a principal form of the constitution of the common, and it is when living labour and language interweave, and define themselves as an ontological machine – it is at that point that the founding experience of the common comes to be a reality. In the *third* place, the *potenza* of the multitude can be revealed on the terrain of the politics of postmodernity, showing how, without the diffusion of knowledge and the emergence of the common, one has none of the conditions whereby a free society can live and reproduce itself. Liberty, in fact, as liberation from command, is materially given only by the development of the multitude and by its constitution as a social body of singularities.

At this point I would like to reply to some of the criticisms that have been directed against this concept of the multitude, but only with the intention of proceeding further with the construction of the concept.

A first grouping of criticisms relates to the interpretation of Foucault and the use of it which is made in the definition of the multitude. These criticisms say that an improper homology is created between the classical concept of the proletariat and that of the multitude. Such a homology – they insist – is dangerous not only ideologically (because it reduces the postmodern onto the modern: this is done, for instance, by the writers of *Spät-modernität*, in other words a group of writers who argue for the dissolution of the modern in our epoch), but also metaphysically, inasmuch as it places the multitude in dialectical opposition with power. I am completely in agreement on the first point. Our era is not 'late modernity' but 'postmodernity'; an epochal break has taken place. However, I do not agree with the second point, because I do not see how, referring to Foucault, one can think that his conception of power excludes antagonism. On the contrary, his conception was never circular, and in his analysis the determinations of power have never been caught in a play of neutralization. It is not true that the relation between micropowers is developed at all the levels of society *without* institutional rupture between the dominators and the dominated. In Foucault there are always material determinations, concrete senses: there is no development which tends towards equilibrium, and thus there is no idealistic schema of historical development. If every concept is fixed in a specific archaeology, it is then, above all, *open* to a genealogy of which we do not know the future. The production of subjectivity, in particular, for all its being produced and determined by power, always develops resistances which open themselves through uncontainable *dispositifs*. The struggles really determine being, they constitute it – and they are always open: only biopower seeks a totalization of them. In reality, theory presents itself as an analysis of a regional system of institutions, struggles, clashes and interplays, and these antagonistic struggles open onto omnilateral horizons. This applies either on the surface of the relations of force or within the ontology of the same. Thus it is in no sense a case of returning to an opposition (in the form of pure exteriority) between power and the multitude, but one of permitting the multitude, in the immeasurable networks that constitute it and in the indefinite strategic determinations that it produces, to free itself from power. Foucault denies the totalization of power, but certainly not the possibility on the part of the subordinated subjects to multiply without end the '*foyers*' of strug-gle' and of production of being. *Foucault is a revolutionary thinker; there is no possibility of reducing his system to a Hobbesian mechanism of equivalent relations.*

A second group of criticisms is directed against the concept of multitude as *potenza* and constituent power. In the first place, criticism is directed against the continued presence, within this powerful conception of the multitude, of a vitalistic idea of the constituent process. The multitude as constituent *potenza* cannot, from this critical point of view, be opposed to the concept of the people as a figure of constituted power: this opposition would render the name of the multitude fragile rather than consistent, virtual rather than real. The critics who assume this point of view maintain that the multitude, once unhooked from the concept of the people and identified as pure *potenza*, risks being reduced to an ethical figure (one of the two sources of ethical creativity, as Bergson considered it). Still around this question (but, so to speak, from the opposite side), the concept of multitude is criti-cized for its inability to become ontologically other, in other words for its inability to present itself as a sufficient critique of sover-eignty. In this critical perspective, the constituent power of the multitude would be attracted by its opposite, and for this reason cannot be assumed as a radical expression of the innovation of reality, nor as a thematic sign of a free people to come. For, as long as the multitude does not express a radicality of foundation which takes it away it from any dialectical exchange with power – they say – it risks being formally included within the political tradition of modernity.

Both these criticisms are lacking in substance. The multitude as *potenza* is not a figure homologous and opposed to the power of exception of modern sovereignty. The constituent power of the multitude is something different – it is not only a political excep-tion, but also a *historical* exception. It is the product of a *radical* temporal *discontinuity*; it is ontological metamorphosis. Thus the multitude presents itself as a powerful singularity which will not allow itself to be caught in the repeated Bergsonian alternative between an eventual and always identical vitalistic function; nor can it be attracted by its overweening opposite, that is, by sovereignty, because it dissolves that concept, through its very existence. This existence of the multitude seeks no grounding outside of itself, but only within its own genealogy. Furthermore, there is no longer a pure or naked foundation, just as there is no longer an outside: these are illusions.

A third group of criticisms, sociological more than philosophical in origin, attacks the concept of multitude, defining it as a 'hypercritical deviation'. What does 'hypercritical' mean? That I leave to the soothsayers. As for the deviation, this would consist basically in assuming that the multitude is installed in a place of refusal, that is, of rupture. For this reason it would be incapable of determining action, indeed it would destroy the very idea of action, because, by definition, starting from a place of absolute refusal, the multitude closes itself to relations and/or mediations with other social actors. In this case the multitude would end up representing a mythical proletariat or an (equally mythical) pure acting subjectivity. It is clear that this critique represents the exact opposite of the critiques which we saw in the first group. In this case too, then, the reply has to recall that the multitude has nothing to do with logics of reasoning subjected to the friend/enemy dyad. The multitude is an ontological name of fullness against emptiness, of production against parasitic leftovers. The multitude knows no instrumental reason, neither within it nor outside it. And, since it is an ensemble of singularities, it is capable of the maximum of mediations and compromising constitutions within itself, when these are emblems of the common (with the multitude operating, anyway, exactly as language operates).

9

LESSON 4

On the Production of Subjectivity: Between War and Democracy

I would like to take the conclusion of the previous lesson as my starting point in introducing a new discussion, on the production of *subjectivity*. My concern is to see whether some of the themes that we have identified can be worked *from below*, so to speak.

The definition of the multitude as the limit of the relationship of capital and of sovereignty, when we relate it to the actual experience of social ontology, means thinking about the new constitution of labour as cooperation, of immaterial labour power as tendency, and of the tendential processes of immaterial labour power towards a hegemony over the entire mode of production. It means initiating a discussion on the tactical and strategic lines that follow from the affirmation of this hegemony. It should be borne in mind that Marx's prophetic forecast instituted the hegemony of intelligence (of labour power) – a general intellect that determined the catastrophic limit of capitalist development.

First, let us define what we mean by *tactical* logic: we need to do this so that we may then be able to see precisely what is meant by subject and production of subjectivity. Tactics is defined first and foremost as practical analysis of the encounter between the subject and the networked infinity of power. The tactics of this subjectivity, having thus emerged, consists in the ability to activate resistance, or rather to *experiment in antagonist forms*, against every point of the structures of power – the relationships, the mechanisms, the technologies that power puts into action – trying to make use of them in order to overturn and empty power itself. We know that we have to move forward within a world made of preconstituted powers: tactics is the native wit of subversive reason.

But before being subversive it is subjective! At this point we have to examine what precisely is meant by subject, subjectivation, ethics and politics. We need to determine the discussion, because it is not enough to found it on the energy that comes from below. This energy too must be *singularized*. So we start from the Foucauldian definitions of subjectivity and of the production of subjectivity. In Foucault, and in French post-structuralism generally, the problem is addressed starting from a critique of the metaphysics of the subject, that is, of the consistent subject, endowed with an absolute freedom, which founds its own autonomy on a metaphysics of the spirit. As we know, the subject has been conceived by modern metaphysics through recourse to consciousness: in this there is not much difference between Descartes and Sartre. Against the philosophies of the subject, Foucault tries to develop an analysis which takes account of the constitution of the subject within the thread of history. The analysis of the constitution of the subject within history (its genealogy) means considering the subject as the product of a series of heterogeneous elements, of determinations that are alien to the subject (qua self-identification or presupposed identity). We must, then, begin to consider the subject in relation to the modalities of consciousness that are specific to each individual age. Each subject is thus the different product of the different technologies that are in play in each given epoch: they are at once those of consciousness and those of power. Every subject is, therefore, the result of a process of subjectivation. Foucault defines three forms of subjectivation. The first form is given through the different modes of knowledge, in other words the different ways in which knowledge reaches the status of science, that is, becomes consolidated as institution. For example, the subject can be constituted through language; but not a generic language, rather the way in which the subject speaks – their grammar, their dialects, the form of their language. The second form is that which has to do with practices of division, i.e.

of classification. In other words those practices which divide the subject within itself, or in relation to other subjects, in order to classify it and turn it into an object: for example the division between the mad and the sane, between the sick and the healthy, between the gentleman and the criminal, etc. The third form is that which is typical of power, which assumes these scientific divisions and classifications in order to overdetermine them through techniques of discipline and control.

At this point, having made a great effort to develop the concept of production of the subject, so to speak, from the outside, Foucault asks: *but this subject, thus constituted, how does it put itself into action? The techniques of power tend to construct the subject, but how does the subject react to these technologies?* This is the crucial point in Foucault's discussion: it is here that the death of God (or of man), which structuralism theorized (and which was the end of metaphysics), is transformed by Foucault into a powerful claim for human action [*agire*]. The deconstructive transition of structuralism is here transformed into a genealogical transition; we are dealing with the genealogy of our existence, hence with an expression of *potenza*, hence with an ethics of existence.

This brings us to the second phase of Foucault's thought, centred on the concept of ethics. How does Foucault move in this regard? First, he makes a distinction between morality and ethics. In general, morality is a set of rules which serve to provide a way of conducting life. In a broad sense, morality is a set of values and rules of action which are proposed to individuals through various prescriptive structures (family, educational institutions, churches, political parties and so on). *Ethics*, on the other hand, *is to do with the way in which people construct themselves as moral subjects*. In Foucault, the term ethics appears for the first time in a truly meaningful way in his review of the *Anti-Oedipus* of Deleuze and Guattari: '*Anti-Oedipus*, if the authors will forgive me, is the first book of ethics that has been written in France for a long time.' Thus ethics is defined here as a line of desire, as a development of *cupiditas*, as constructive *potenza*.

In his book on the use of pleasures, Foucault develops this constructive methodology. Articulating a long analysis of how the Greeks and Christians constructed the subject in real terms, Foucault argues that on the one hand the search for happiness and on the other the subjugation of the person to God constitute its central pole. On the one hand the *aphrodisiac* of classical civilization; on the other the medieval 'control of the flesh'. What is interesting here is not so much the object – the classical aphrodisiac or the medieval flesh – but rather the ability to construct the subject through practices of power. Which, as it turns out, are practices of subjectivation. We construct ourselves as humans, as subjects. The question, therefore, is not simply that of power and its ability to construct subjectivity, but also, and above all, that of the reactions to power, of resistance on the part of the subject: one resists only if one has the ability to construct oneself as a subject, and it is only in these terms that one can go on to discuss constituent strategies, genealogical constitution of the subject and exodus.

Take the example of the Seattle revolt (1999). This is obviously not something that Foucault could have discussed because it was after his time, but we can still interpret it in a Foucauldian sense. The meaning of Seattle is effectively the *production of an ethics against power*. In a Foucauldian sense, and certainly in a bio-political sense, Seattle reveals a radical modification in our ways of conceiving life, our ways of speaking: it is the moment at which one passes from morality to ethics, in which a multitude of singularities reveals itself as a subjective force. *It is an event.*

There is another path that can be taken, and which leads us to the same conclusions reached by Foucault. This is a path far more within the paths of social philosophy, of sociology and political philosophy in the strict sense: it is the path that started within the *reform of Marxism* and which, in my own case, I have tried to develop from within workerism [*operaismo*]. In this case, too, it was a project of overturning, so to speak, the point of view by which categories were defined, in other words of constituting the categories from below, submitting them to the rules of action, of collective praxis. From consciousness to morality and from morality to ethics, this seems to be the path that was taken also within workerism. Here the central theme is the dimension of time. Marxism told us that value is time. The law of value was a kind of projection of human activity reduced to labour. On this point Marxism presented itself as a twofold opening. On the one hand, the projection of human activity in labour was considered alienating, or rather alienation was precisely that abstraction of human activity. From another point of view, Marxism presented itself as a technology of transformation; it proposed itself as an operativity within, and on the concrete time of, production: the critique of alienation was matched, constructively, by the technology of planning. In the reform of Marxism there was an initial phase of studies which examined the problem of dissolving that temporality (substance of the law of the value) which presented itself in objectivist terms. The first problem was therefore that of dissolving objective temporality and of relating back to the subject, to make of temporality a stage-setting within which the subject constructed a world. To snatch Marxism back from its scientific status and restore it to its utopian, or rather ethical, possibility was a first essential passage. The question of the subject thus became central to Marxist philosophy and to revolutionary practice. To put it in extreme terms, in relation to planning, the problem was that of uncoupling the conception of time-value from its measures and its structures. It was therefore necessary to oppose, to the time of planning, a new dimension of temporality, uncoupled from repetitivity and from extreme socialist objectivism and dogmatism. *The opposition consisted in the ability to propose a new way of living and enjoying time.*

The importance of this aspect in the thinking of Marxist reform cannot be overestimated. Already in the 1970s, faced with the highly developed capacities for controlling temporality in heavy industry (in Taylorism and in labour processes in general, whatever the form of management, whether it was liberal or socialist), we saw a militant critique emerging: it identified an opposite temporality – the time of rupture and innovation, not a repetitive and planned constitution of time but the *time of innovation*, and thus a different temporality, which could open to the future. It was no accident that this new conception of time made it possible to draw up a *new vision of the common*, precisely as cooperation, and a new conception of the multitude, precisely as an ensemble of proliferating singularities. This new social ontology permitted us to produce 'ethical' subjects (to use Foucauldian terms), subjects which activate themselves within a different practice of time, a time that becomes excessive and beyond measure from the point of view of its measurement (in other words, seen from the outside) or excedence (when lived time is seen from inside, from below, from that original construction of being which is our productive life).

The same could also be said as regards the definition of space. Here, too, we need to address the spatial dimension in a new way, different from that of the past. *The spatiality of the past is a spatiality that has been dissolved.* This is not an apologia for the 'global village', nor are we flattening space and/or dispersing it in pure communicative forms; rather, we want to identify the new forms of relating and the new modes of production that are brought into being on the basis of this transformation/dissolution. It means reconstructing these spaces. And reconstructing these spaces means reconstructing them in ethical ways, by dissolving the structures of power that dominated these spaces. *Constructing* different spaces in an ethical sense thus means *reinventing them.*

At this point, however, a pause for thought would be in order. All this is going too smoothly. We are describing a possible New Age – but this possibility is far from real. Over these times, over these spaces, over these productions of subjectivity, extremely heavy functions of control are being extended. *And yet* our illusion, this possibility, is more real than we might think: and there is an absolutely monstrous fact that gives us the proof of the effectiveness of the illusion, and it is that *war is becoming the technology of power*, a technology geared to dominating or to blocking this transformation. When we spoke of discipline and control as techniques geared to command over different social compositions of labour, we were referring to the development of methods for control over the population. There was – we said – a certain match between the technologies of government and the forms of subjectivity. So now we need to understand how war, today, represents a form of control geared to the new subjectivity, to the new form of labour, and thus to the new production of subjectivity.

To repeat: when we spoke of discipline as a technique matched to the production of the subject as a massified individuality, and when, in what we called the second phase of the era of heavy industry (which was also the phase of the mass management of populations, and thus also of fascisms and of the development/ crisis of colonialism), we saw matching methods of control (methods of control in the real sense of the word, such as control over populations) which, again, were a match between techno-logies of governance and the forms of subjectivity, of the production of subjectivity. Thus far everything seems to work. But to say that war nowadays is a form of command, just as discipline and control were the characteristic forms of the first and second phases of heavy industry, and that war is a direct function of bio-political control, is a statement that needs to be handled with care. I recall saying in an earlier lesson that war intervened in a linear fashion to complete the models of control, in other words that *war has to be understood as an extension of the models of discipline and control.* The production of the power of control is like a Russian doll: in historical order, it produces disciplinary power, then power of control, and today, probably, war. In effect, if we consider the doll today for what it currently represents, the order is reversed: in other words, war contains control and discipline. *The form of imper-ial biopower today is a war that contains control and discipline within it.* Whereas in the modern tradition war was defined as the continuation of politics by other means, today it seems that the aphorism has been turned on its head: war is the foundation of politics, it is the basic way through which politics is formed. Already Foucault had proposed this reversal. But to say that war is the foundation of politics means to take as implicit a further transition, namely to recognize within war those capacities for producing subjectivity which discipline and control possessed. *War*, at this point, is not purely destructive power, but rather a *regulating power*, which is constituent, teleological, and thus inscribed within duration as a processual activity and at the same time inscribed in space as a selective and hierarchizing activity. War is long and never-ending. Furthermore, it is selective and hierarchical; it designates spaces and borders. There we have the definition of war in postmodernity.

We could take this further. In modernity, war created order through peace. In Hobbes we see war as a conflictual moment of all against all and only at the end, through peace, was order delivered up. *Today, on the contrary, order is not arrived at through the ending of war, but through a continuous promotion of war.* It is through this permanent action of war that the functions of control and discipline are proposed and applied. If order is not arrived at through bringing war to an end, but by promoting discipline and control through a continuous promotion of war, *if war is itself the very form of biopower*, then the question of defining the enemy becomes central. Here the *enemy* needs to be continuously con-structed and invented; paradoxically, he cannot be defeated, or, if he has been defeated, another enemy must immediately be found. The enemy is public danger, he is the symptom of a disorder needing to be ordered. In other words, he is *the threat that is posed by the very presence of the multitude.* This threat must in some way be disciplined and controlled. Every subject can be an enemy of the Empire. Every subject can be a public danger and *qua* multitude of singularities, can be defined as a limit of power.

However, faced with this situation, and reconceptualizing war, the question arises: *can power destroy its subject?* The levels reached by the technologies of death are indeed capable of bringing about total destruction. But this destruction is stupid from the point of view of power itself. In fact power is a relationship, and it is this to the extent that it has subjects; in the same way, capital exists only as a relationship that has consumers. If imperial power were today to trigger its entire power of destruction, this would be a suicide for power. This means that we have a growing contradiction between the *dispositifs* of war and those of life, in other words on one side the mechanisms of destruction and on the other the mechanisms of economics, communications etc. Janus-faced, you could say. So I say again, given this huge threat of destruction, paradoxically war becomes less and less destructive, because in effect it is no longer war and has become an action of policing. If we assume the premises of *Empire*, the thing seems fairly clear: *in a world that no longer has an outside, war is always internal, and thus it is less and less war and more and more policing.*

(Here we should note that the *reduction* of war to policing, that is, to a capacity for establishing order, *does not deny but on the contrary exasperates* the ontological character of war, in other words it effectively reveals it to us as a capacity for producing and/or designing orders of subjectivity. When war becomes less and less like war and more and more like policing, in any event the dilution of the war function and the rise of the police function have ontological stigmata. I am not able to say to what extent this is conditioned by the fact that there are formidable nuclear arsenals planted in the bowels of the Earth and that, every so often, we hear mad voices discussing the possible use of these weapons. In any event, the intermixing of war and policing still carries with it the possibility of nuclear terror. And correctly, for at least fifty years, pacifism has been denouncing it. In short, when war and policing are joined together, under that cover there is a terrible indistinction, fed by that nuclear potential that introduces every possibility of terror.)

If, in the logical order of the Russian doll, war contains within it control and discipline, then we have to *assume this continuity* also *as a trace of identification in the forms of industrial production* which *sustain, and are interwoven with, our present forms of life*. If command over individuals is entrusted to war, to control and to discipline, if we see control as being inherent to the modern and postmodern forms of production, then what are the other, more specific, forms in which war presents itself as a form of productive life? What comes to mind is those productions which have as their reference point (consumer or victim) the multitude – hence the biological technologies, chemical technologies, and of course computer science technologies. War produces means of destruction that affect the multitude, the ensemble of singularities, and is based therefore on the relationship between biopower, big industry and social production.

Furthermore, in examining postmodern war we find ourselves facing another extremely important element: the formation of juridical orders. War produces its law-courts. The definition of the enemy involves consequent definitions of specific sanctions that have nothing to do with the old international law. Behind the courts, then, come the concentration camps, and the re-emergence of ways of treating bodies which in modernity used to be called torture but today are called psychological conditioning. We have to understand how all this is developing in totalitarian ways. With that we can complete the picture. This power of war is defined, in fact, by something absolutely characteristic, its *asymmetric* character. Asymmetric means that it is never a war between equals, but a war which comes from on high, which uses more powerful means, and which is a permanent state of exception. Now we have arrived at the point. Summing up the characteristics of war that we have outlined, we find that war is defined as having the forms of power *par excellence*: it produces forms of life, forms of relations. The great difference between this war and the others is that this is not only a foundation of politics but is also a foundation of the biopolitical, of the vital order, and this inasmuch as it is inscribed in time and space, that is, inscribed in an action which is infinite and in a space which is a formative possibility of networks. If peace is no longer distinct from war, then war and peace merge into one single matrix, which is biopolitics. *Postmodern war is something less than modern war, but it is also something more than modern policing. Postmodern war has become – monstrously – a kind of machine that is productive of the social.*

There are many aspects which indicate this transition from the war of modernity to postmodern war. We need only think of the reform of the world's armies, carried out massively after 1989 (the end of the Cold War). Armies are no longer institutions designed for high-intensity combat, but small units capable of military missions anywhere in the world, being sent promptly wherever they are needed but also carrying out intelligence missions and providing aid and assistance (NGO type work entrusted to the military). What we have here is a restructuring of the army as a fundamental operator in the area of sociality. This merging between war and policing gives us an image of the panoply of the forms of imperial governance. Another example is the virtualization of postmodern war. It would like to be war without bodies, or rather without losses on the side of imperial power. It considers the loss of one soldier as a crime of *lèse majesté*. The soldier has in fact become a public official, a direct representative of authority. Here, all convention-type legislation – for instance the Geneva conventions on the treatment of prisoners – is necessarily and unavoidably blown out. As for the enemy dead, or the decimated civilian populations, they fall under the heading of 'collateral damage'. We could cite examples from the war in the Balkans, the war in Afghanistan, or the other wars that are under way, and we would find that all this has come about fully and completely. But, for the moment, what we have said thus far will suffice.

I shall conclude with a further reflection on the meaning of *11 September*. Posing the question does not mean that 11 September has changed everything: as far as I am concerned, it only made explicit what was already implicit and ripe in the epochal transition of the preceding decade. However, it is beyond doubt that after 11 September everything *seems* to be changed: this is a statement that power makes of itself, as if it had been forced into an acceleration of its expressions in terms of command and repression. However, there is again the awareness on the part of all of us that we are in a situation of war; what we felt confusedly throughout the 1990s has now become obvious. The formation of Empire has led us into war, a war that is regulatory, in which what is being constituted is mechanisms of discipline and control – for example in the war in Yugoslavia. It is through war that new borders are traced, new power élites and new agglomerates of subjectivity are produced; it is through war that new institutions are brought into being, such as the international courts, and that the mechanisms of policing intervention are perfected. In short, it is through war that the material forces come into being which constitute Empire, which determine its hierarchies and the inner circulation of powers.

The war in Afghanistan revealed further modifications in the figure of sovereignty. Already before 11 September, Michael Hardt and I had introduced the *distinction between the Byzantine model and the Latin model of Empire.* When we spoke of the Byzantine model, we were thinking of an imperial form in which a hugely present feature was the transcendence of power. Byzantium is a power that represents itself as untouchable sacrality. Look at the apses of Byzantine basilicas: in the centre sits the imperial divinity, the *Pantocrator*, and around him are the twelve apostles and the signs of the apocalypse. In the face of this transcendental untouchability of power, the multitude is distanced and repressed: it is the very imaginary of the exodus that is hit here. Thus we find ourselves today facing the imperial dynamics of a Byzantine type. These were conceived before 11 September and, when 11 September happened, it brought them fully to light. So, if we are indeed on this terrain, we will have to say that so-called American unilateralism signals the way forward for the entire political class of imperial capital; *American unilateralism is the Byzantine representation of a general line, a line which is pivoted on war.*

How are we to oppose this enormity of power? I agree with those who say that only bodies can create an opposition to Byzantine power. After Genoa, *the conviction that only bodies can resist has become general.* But we should be careful when we talk about resistance of bodies because, for example, a suicide bomber is also a body that resists. Our problem is obviously not that of the suicide bomber: we want to exercise a resistance which is at the same time an affirmation both of life and of desire. War cannot be opposed through war. True opposition to war can only come about through affirming the primacy of the multitude in the production of subjectivity: this means opposing ourselves to the blockage of production of subjectivity that war seeks to impose. War cannot be blocked except through the constitutive power of the multitude.

This observation needs to be fine-tuned, however. In opposing war, the problem is not simply that of trusting the ontological accumulation of the subjectivity of the multitude; we also have to view this ontological accumulation against each of the obstacles that war raises (in the indifference that we now find between military actions and police repression, between high- and low-intensity wars). *How do we deal with the asymmetry of power? How do we measure the limit beyond which imperial power cannot go, except at the risk of its own suicide?*

Resistance of bodies, we said. Now, the resistance of bodies means the biopolitical empowering of bodies: we have to gamble on the possibility of resistance and on technologies of resistance that make themselves absolute. Do you remember the film *Brazil?* It is a celebration of a resistance that involves human metamorphosis, which powerfully mixes mobility and joy, which constructs common networks and invents languages that puncture the systems of domination. I believe that these behaviours are to be found today in the practice of the movements, and they need to be generalized.

The transition we are living through is decisive. We have said that the war we are living at present is an *ordinative imperial war*. But it is not only this: it is also *a war of transition* between different eras, just like the Thirty Years War in the years between 1618 and 1648, which turned Central Europe upside down. Germany lost two thirds of its population in a war which appeared in formal terms to be one between Catholics and Protestants, but which in fact was the decisive moment of the anti-Renaissance counter-revolution. The humanistic and libertarian utopia was defeated, and out of the ruins of the Republic was constructed the absolutist state. The juridical construction of the sovereign, modern and absolutist state represents the defeat of Renaissance republicanism. We must take care that this does not happen again today, with the construction of Empire becoming the end of democracy. The imperial ruling class tells us that we have entered a Thirty Years War. It is their war, and the choices left to us are resistance and exodus.

Resistance and exodus are a construction which is at once internal and external, an ethical constitution and a practical resistance.

To summarize what has been said in this fourth lesson: we have tried to define a strategy of the production of subjectivity which avoids getting entangled with power, and which culminates in exodus. In my Macchina tempo *(Feltrinelli, Milan, 1982 [published in* Time for Revolution, Continuum International, *London, 2003]; the central section was published in* La costituzione del tempo, *Manifestolibri, Rome, 1999), I identified the ontological difference which makes it possible to nurture, within the autonomy of productive temporality, a strategy of exodus. This perspective was also developed in* Kairos, Alma Venus, Multitudo *(Manifestolibri, Rome, 2000)* [Kairos, Alma Venus, Multitudo, *in* Time For Revolution, Continuum, *London, 2003].* Here, in this lesson, the strategic point of view is accompanied by a tactical one: the logic of tactics is the emptying, shifting, utilization, and* destabilization of imperial power *by whatever means. The production of subjectivity feeds on tactical moments and strategic moments, on the destabilization of imperial power and on the structuring of the* potenza *of the multitude.*

It is exactly against this potenza *that Empire (in its figure which is now definitively Byzantine) poses war as the means to complete the production of its power. War represents, simultaneously, the continuity and the circularity of the production of power:* discipline, control and war *are* complementary *and successive moments in the expression of power.* But war contains and includes them all: *discipline and control are absorbed within the acceleration of the time of power that war makes possible. It is starting from this ontological determination that the concept of war has been profoundly modified, both in its philosophical conception and in its military theory. For the military theory, see A.* Joxe, Empire of Disorder, Semiotext(e), *New York, 2002; R. Di Nunzio and U. Rapetto,* Le nuove guerre, *Rizzoli, Milan 2001; and, above all, Qiao Liang and Wang Xiangsui,* Unrestricted Warfare: China's Master Plan to Destroy America, *NewsMax Media, Florida, 1999. For the philosophical point of view see Carlo Galli,* La guerra, globale, Laterza, *Roma–Bari, 2002.*

10

Counterpower*

I   When people talk in general terms about 'counterpower' they are actually talking about three separate things: *resistance* against the old power; *insurrection*; and *a* potenza *which is constitutve of a new power*. Resistance, insurrection and constituent power are the threefold figure of the single essence of counterpower.

We know more or less accurately what *resistance* is, since in daily life a great majority of social subjects practise it. In productive activities, against the boss; in activities of social reproduction, against the authorities that regulate and control life (in the family, paternalism . . .); in social communication, against the values and systems that lock experience and language into repetition and push them towards non-meaning. Resistance interacts harshly, but also creatively, with command at nearly all the levels of lived social life.

As for *insurrection*, this is not so easy to experience: but in the course of a generation (and, in the past two centuries, every thirty of years or so) people have experienced it. For us, insurrection means the form taken by a mass movement of resistance when it becomes active over a short period of time, or concentrates its energies on certain defined and determining objectives: it represents the mass innovation of a common

* Previously published in *Situaciones*, no. 3, Buenos Aires 2001.

political discourse. Insurrection pulls together the various forms
of resistance into a single knot, homologizes them, arranges them
like an arrow which, in an original manner, succeeds in crossing
the limit of the given social organization, of constituted power.
It is an event.

Constituent power is the *potenza* to give form to the innovation
that resistance and uprising have produced, and to give them a
new and adequate historical form which is teleologically effective.
Where, on the one hand, the insurrection pushes resistance to
become innovation (and thus expresses the eruptive productivity
of *living labour*), constituent power gives form to this expression
(accumulates the mass *potenza* of living labour into a new project
of life, into a new potential of civilization). And, whereas the insurrection is a weapon that destroys the life-forms of the enemy,
constituent power is the force that positively organizes new
schemas of life and mass enjoyment of life.

II In the political language of the traditional Left, the term
counterpower has more precise and limited characteristics: often
it is seen simply as the practice of resistance, and sometimes as
its organization . . . and that's it! This precise and limited definition is a mistake: not because, often, things effectively do not
proceed like that, and not only because the nexus that connects
resistance to further stages in the expression of counterpower is
visible only with difficulty – but because, if one does not recognize
the implicit interlinking between resistance, insurrection and constituent power in every figure of counterpower, then one risks
neutralizing those same components, emptying them of effectiveness or even handing them over unsuspectingly to the dominant
power. The fact is that, in highly complex societies such as postmodern society, resistance, if taken by itself, can operate in a
vacuum, or, worse, can be manipulated within operations of sys-
temic circulation that only the recomposition of a global point of
view of counterpower can interrupt. Thus the insurrectional
dynamics, however generous it may be, can become useless, or
even harmful, if it is not commensurate with the potentialities of
the masses; it risks, therefore, running aground in the swamps
of terrorism, when its incidence has not become (through preceding phases of resistance) mass-based, and when its constituent
imagination has not become *hegemonic*. As for constituent power,

its effectiveness only becomes obvious when it is consistently implanted in an irreversible process of transformation of ways of life and of the affirmation of desires for liberation. From yet another point of view, however, from a point of view that does not privilege the separation of the different components of counterpower but rather exalts their connectedness, there can be effects which are ambiguous and even negative. This can be the case when one considers counterpower in the temporal dimension, and here in a perspective that is strongly foreshortened: then the nexus between resistance, insurrectionary activity and constituent power can be described in a dialectic of *immediacy*, in which each single moment (together with the activities and functions and determinations of counterpower) becomes ungraspable, incapable of execution . . . It is usually when one finds oneself in situations in which organization (and reflection) is surrogated by the spontaneity of the movements that such *impasses* come about – with consequences that are often disastrous. Nights in which 'all cows are grey' are always disastrous – and you can go crazy there. When resistance, uprising and constituent power are lived (immediately) in a time which is compact and without articulations, 'the beautiful soul' prevails over critical thought, and concrete operativity is rendered stupid by over-enthusiasm . . . Machiavelli tells of the anti-Medici revolt of the Boscoli, a revolt that was humanist and most generous in spirit (he was not a participant, but was caught up in the events): he tells us that such adventurous and disastrously ineffective experiences of counterpower are unacceptable, because they are contracted into a time and a passion lacking reflection.

III   It is not only this indistinction of temporality that destroys the effectiveness of counterpower and perhaps also its very definition: there can be also a distortion of the space within which counterpower is exercised and develops itself. To clarify this point, let us return to the basic definition of counterpower and try to enrich it.

Resistance has – within the total process of counterpower – a principal function, which is that of *destructuring* the opposing power. It is a difficult task, a continuous digging, a putting into crisis of the single relationships and the singular compromises/ manipulations which in every angle of social space constitute the totality of command. What is in play here is counterposed micropowers: to throw them off-balance and sabotage their eventual accord in order to insert elements of rupture into the global structure of the system – this is one task of resistance . . . The more mass-based it is, the more effective will be the work of destructuring, of emptying the mediations and institutional recompositions of meaning, and therefore the more potent will be the action of resistance. As for insurrectionary activity, it has as its task to block the reaction of the existing power and to force it into the defensive. (I also mean that even if insurrectionary activity does not achieve its central aim or objective immediately it is nonetheless useful: it can prevent constituted power from repairing the damage that the resistance succeeds in doing – and continues to do – to its structure. The enemy front is thus further damaged.) When capitalist power (which is the enemy today) is analysed, we see that on the one hand it continuously structures life and society, and on the other hand it makes specific interventions at points where it needs to stabilize its dominion. Capitalist power, therefore, closely articulates on the one hand the structuring of the world of life and production and, on the other, the guarantees required for its reproduction. Counterpower, in order to exercise itself and to be effective, must therefore have a *double aspect*: on the one hand it has to dig into, continually dismantle, and undermine the social structure of power; on the other, it has to intervene in offensive fashion into/against the operations of stabilization which power continually tries to effect, and which constitute the specificity of its capacity for government. The 'counterpower' that destructures must also be matched by a 'counter-government' that *destabilizes*. Thirdly, there is the action of constituent power. This is what increases – over the whole terrain of power, and against it – *the alternative imagination*: it means thinking out, all together, the future becoming of the multitude as *potenza*, as a new form of production and reproduction of life, and of the struggle against death. This imagination must be a living force within the resistance and the militant experience of the uprising: just as the behaviours of resistance and uprising nourish and renew the constituent imagination.

But let us return now to the question which was our starting point, in other words the possibility that power had of re-territorializing (and therefore blocking into a closed space and eventually neutralizing) the force of counterpower, when it does not present itself in the full articulation of its functions and dislocations. It seems to us that the problem is fairly obvious: neither resistance, nor insurrectional activity, nor constituent power will be able to avoid manoeuvres of recuperation and castration if they fail to develop mechanisms of strategy for themselves.

There is, of course, a long-standing tradition of capitalist power that guarantees efficacy in the recuperation and neutralization of counterpower: it is the tradition of *constitutionalism*. The recuperation of counterpower becomes possible in constitutionalism because resistance, uprising and constituent power here come to be reduced to a simple juridical claim, and are thus configured as *dialectical* elements, as participants in the democratic . . . synthesis of the system. In constitutionalism, counterpower is re-territorialized, closed into a space that is already organized by a single principle of command, namely exploitation and hierarchy.

But counterpower is the opposite of all that!

IV   In order to approach the practice and concept of counterpower in the distinct complexity of its figures and in the originality of its *potenza*, we must now stress another point: the *non-homology* of *mass* counterpower with constituted power.

In the political theory of Spinoza, the impossibility of the homologation of power and counterpower is posed particularly strongly and clearly. Spinoza lists for us the familiar classical theory of forms of government: the government of the one (monarchy), the government of the few (aristocracy), and the government of the multitude (democracy) . . . But next to democracy he adds 'absolute' – and out comes 'absolute democracy', in other words a form of government that has nothing to do with others, because the multitude, when it commands over itself, goes beyond all the other forms of organized social existence, and does not present itself as a political theory of a determination, but of being *without* determinations, absolute everywhere and without limits. It is therefore perfectly possible to conceive of a form that has nothing to do with monarchic power or aristocratic power – and nothing to do with democratic power either, when this is still one of the figures of power rather than being a function of the *potenza* of the multitude.

To put it even more clearly: it is necessary for the activity of counterpower *not* to have as its aim *the replacement of existing power*. On the contrary, it must propose different forms and expressions of mass liberty. If we want to define counterpower, within and against the present postmodern forms of power, we must insist continually and powerfully on the fact that, through counterpower, we do not want to conquer and to get our hands on the old power, but to develop a new *potenza* of life, organization and production. Counterpower knows neither *telos* nor *Aufhebung*: it does not produce development of preconceived essences, but simply lives and produces life.

V In the traditions of the communist and labour movements, counterpower as a concept has functioned in highly ambiguous terms, with multiple applications.

In Marx there is a teleology of proletarian counterpower that functions both within the temporal coordinate of development (communism is necessary) and within the spatial coordinate (it is within the perspective of the globalization of capital and of the construction of the world market that the revolution imposes itself). In Lenin, while the spatial tendency still shows itself as necessary and indefinite, the time and the moment of the revolutionary exercise of counterpower become essential: it is within the moment, the occasion, the weak point of the chain of capitalist exploitation that the revolutionary project grasps the *kairos* and innovates history. Rosa Luxemburg, on the other hand, remains closed within a powerful temporal teleology (revolution as necessary), but identifies, at the limit of the capitalist market and thus within spatial marginality, the occasion of crisis which makes the revolutionary process possible. Whereas for Lenin imperialism is the highest point of capitalist development, and consequently the point at which the working class can be strongest, and which must be felled with one blow, in Rosa Luxemburg imperialism opens to the weaker, more open and more critical points of capitalist development – it is here that it is possible to begin to construct resistance and uprising – thereby carrying constituent power and revolution towards the centre of command, in a destructive advance through the enemy system. Finally, the anarchists: they have always refused to define a time or a space as privileged moments of uprising; they live in the chaos of the world of exploitation, illustrating destructively its institutions (sometimes in very rich ways . . . we need only think of the notion of the 'abolition of the state' which they introduced into the political theory of revolution) or thinking that there are one or thousands of spaces and times of revolt . . . It is a pity that the anarchist conception has never been attentive to the issue of homology with the state . . . so that it reproduces in its concept of insurrection and in that of the abolition of the state a revolutionary imprint that is fiercely *empty* of alternative proposals and full of resentment.

Obviously we could continue narrating these ideologies. Far more important, however, is to show that the inability to give the concept of counterpower a figure that is non-homologous to constituted power derives above all from an implicit premise, or rather from *the latent homology* (the skeleton in the cupboard) of the economic model which, precisely in a homogeneous way, stands behind the thought and the practice of power, and the thought and practice of counterpower: namely *the model of capitalist development*. It is this that determines, with the homology, with the unicity of the concept, the teleology, the sameness of strategic designs even in the extreme difference of moves and tactics, even in total enmity. Because the capitalist model is dialectical.

VI So at this point how can we finalize a definition of 'counterpower'? There is an ontological definition: this consists in emphasizing that insurrectionary resistance and activities represent constituent powers, latent but active, all the more so as the control of the movements (the efficacious formation of imperial control over labour power, over its dynamics and its displacements) becomes global. It is very true that struggles no longer succeed in communicating, and that, if they do succeed, it is at an ideological rather than a political level (from the Palestinian Intifada to the Los Angeles revolt, from French strikes of 1995 to Chiapas, from the Indonesian and South Korean revolts to the 'Sem tierra' landless workers' movement in Brazil . . .): nevertheless, the struggles as extreme and powerful danger are always present, obsessively pressing on the capitalist definition of development. The political guarantee of capitalist development has to answer this challenge. The state (this is also true in the imperial phase) is organized in order to control and to repress counterpower. Thus we can understand why global 'collective capital' has today decided to use the phrase 'the people [*popolo*] of Seattle' to describe those strong and durable counterpowers which in every corner of the planet are emerging, proud and just, into the light of history. (The phrase is used as a way of disarming them, as if they were just revindications of rights and not expressions of *potenza*.) No, it is not the icons of Pope Gapon now set up in Seattle, as they already are elsewhere in that century of revolution and of class struggle that we have emerged from – it is certainly not these symbols that are capable of blocking the force of ontological transformation which is emanating from counterpower . . . This counterpower becomes increasingly able to affect the structures of the balance of power, as the capitalist regime comes increasingly to be seen in terms of 'corruption' – in other words, in that omnipresent and delirious crisis which follows on the fall of every criterion of measure, of every real sign of value, in the construction of global market and imperial command. Here post-Fordism, Empire, liberalism and globalization and . . . post-modernity begin to coincide. In this picture, then, counterpower is the only force that exalts the representation of reality. Ontology is moved by its wind. The history of the world is its expression. The revolution is, perhaps, its outcome.

VII   What might be the meaning of counterpower in the society of imperial globalization? It is hard to imagine counterpower becoming effective on a national basis, that is, within the framework of the nation-state which the Empire is embracing within its dialectics of strategic control. Moreover, imperial power is trying to constitutionalize, in other words to co-opt and control, the more significant phenomena of resistance taking place on the surface of the planet. The acknowledgement of the 'people of Seattle', or of the more important NGOs, enters into this dynamics of a relative constitutionalization of a new 'civil society' . . . What mystifications! A true counterpower, today, thus has to avoid moving at a purely national level, and has to avoid being absorbed into the ranks of the new imperial constitutionalism.

So how are we to move forward?

To answer this question, it would be good to reflect on some experiences which, while they offer no certainties, do indicate possible paths that could be followed in the building of counterpower today. The first experience is that (which remains as valid as ever) of building resistance from the bottom, through a rooting in social and productive situations. In other words, we have to continue, through resistance and *militancy*, with destructuring the dominant power in the places where it is accumulated and centralized and from which it declares its hegemony. Resisting it from the bottom means extending and building into the resistance the 'common' networks of knowledge and action, against the privatization of command and wealth. It means breaking the hard lines of exploitation and exclusion. It means constructing common languages, in which the alternative of a free life and the struggle against death can emerge victorious. In the recent decades there have been struggles which have shown these objectives, and a movement of the multitudes which was radically dedicated to these objectives: the Paris struggles of winter 1995 were exemplary from this point of view. But in order to become strategies these struggles need to find connections world-wide, a global dimension of circulation. They need to be supported by material *potenze*, specifically, by a labour power that moves through lines of cultural and working emigration, both material and immaterial – in short, by a powerful and radical world-political exodus. Imperial power thus has to be opposed by a counterpower operating at the level of Empire.

It is strange, but interesting and highly suggestive, to remember how Che Guevara had intuited something of what we are saying here. Namely that proletarian internationalism has to be transformed into a great political and physical *métissage*, which can unite what used to be the nations, and today are the multitudes, into one single struggle for liberation.

11

What to Make of 'What Is to Be Done?' Today: The Body of General Intellect*

> The weak point of the imperialist chain is the point where
> the working class is strongest.
>
> Mario Tronti, *Lenin in England*, 1964

The biopolitical face of Leninism

'To speak of Lenin is to speak of the conquest of power. There is
no point in looking at his thinking and his actions from any other
point of view (regardless of whether you like them or not): Lenin's
sole theme is that of the conquest of power.' Thus does Western
political science render homage to Lenin, paradoxically praising
his 'sombre grandeur' . . . Maybe Mussolini and Hitler even
dreamed of being Lenin? However, at the end of the civil war of
the twentieth century it is in these terms that bourgeois political
science grants recognition to Lenin, to the victor of October 1917,
to the man of timely decision and firm resolve.

It is a repellent form of recognition, however.

What does the 'seizure of power' mean in revolutionary
Marxism? In the workers' movement of the 1800s and 1900s and
in the communist movement the 'seizure of power' is inseparable

* First published in *Contretemps*, No. 2, Paris, September 2001.

from the project for the 'abolition of the state'. Lenin is no exception. His extraordinary venture is inseparable from that project. This fact in itself is enough to place a thousand miles between what Lenin did and the ambiguous assessment that bourgeois political science makes of him. Certainly, Lenin's project was only half successful: it conquered power but it did not abolish the state. And certainly that state, which was supposed to perish, went on to become so strong and ferocious as to dissolve, for whole generations of militants for communism, any hope of ever being able to combine the taking of power and the abolition of the state. Nevertheless the question remains . . . To begin to speak of Lenin again means asking whether it is possible to re-embark on the path which can, at the same time, subvert the statist order of existing things and invent a world of freedom and equality, destroying the metaphysical *arche* of the Western world, both as a principle of authority and as a mechanism of social exploitation, political hierarchy and command over production.

Having posed the problem, another note should be added immediately, following on from the acknowledgement that capitalist power is indistinguishably state command and a social structure for exploitation, and that the revolution, when it is communist, attacks and destroys both. The note is that, for Lenin (as for revolutionary Marxism in general), the communist struggle is biopolitical. This is because it invests every aspect of life, but, above all, because the revolutionary political will of communists addresses itself directly to the *bios*, criticizes it, constructs it, transforms it. Lenin carries political science outside of every idealistic simplification, every idea of '*raison d'état*', outside of every illusory definition of the political in bureaucratic or decisionist terms. But still more radically: outside of every separation between the political and the social and human. As a political thinker, Lenin begins by freeing the analysis of the state from the theory of forms of government (that ancient theory, endlessly repeated and always mystificatory); he then proposes the analysis of the political outside of the disingenuous hypotheses which see it as mirroring economic forms, and he does this by freeing himself from chiliastic impulses and secular utopias which, around a hypothesis of revolution, might confuse the view. Quite the contrary, he mixes, hybridizes, overturns, revolutionizes all of these theories: what must always emerge victorious is the proletarian political will, in which bodies and reason, life and passions, rebellion and project can be constituted into a biopolitical subject – the subject which is the 'working class', its 'vanguard', the spirit of the proletariat *in* its body.

Although in many respects Rosa Luxemburg is a long way from Lenin, here, as regards the biopolitical nature of the communist project, she is at her closest. In differing ways, Luxemburg's curve and Lenin's straight line intersect in assuming the life of the masses and the full articulation of their needs as a physical, bodily potential which is the only thing which can provide the necessary basis and content for the abstraction and violence of revolutionary intellectuality. This advance of the political ontology of communism is extremely mysterious – but it is also very real – it reveals, with its biopolitical aspect, the extraordinary modernity of communist thought, in the corporeal fullness of the freedom it expresses and seeks after. Lenin is completely within all this, in this materialism of bodies in the process of liberating themselves, in the materiality of a life which finds renewal through (and only through) revolution. Lenin is the revolutionary invention of a body, not an apologia for the autonomy of the political.

Lenin beyond Lenin

But what is the real meaning of exploitation and of the struggle against exploitation *today* (not yesterday and not a century ago)? What is this body today, which has revolutionized itself in the adventures and the civil wars of the twentieth century? What is the new body of the struggle for communism?

Already in the early 1960s (and since then with growing intensity) these questions were coming to the fore. Without any great possibilities of resolution, but in the belief that, on these questions, Lenin should not merely be interrogated with exegetic fidelity, but should also be re-proposed – going, as we used to say, 'beyond Lenin'.

So the first problem was that of preserving the meaning of Leninism within the transformation of the world of production, within the relationships of power that characterized it, and within the changes suffered by the social subjects. A second problem, generated together with the first, was that of rendering Leninism (that is, the question of organization for anti-capitalist revolution and for the destruction of the state) adequate for the present realities of the organization of production and for the pressures of the newly emerging subjects. This means, therefore, asking how the conquest of power and the abolition of the state might be possible in a historical period (here I anticipate a vital point) of the hegemony of capital over general intellect.

Everything has changed. Compared with the realities lived and theorized by Lenin, production and command today invest a new technical and political composition of the workforce.

The experience of exploitation has been completely transformed by all this. The fact is that the nature of productive labour today is fundamentally immaterial, and cooperation in production is entirely social. This has the result that labour is co-extensive with life and cooperation is co-extensive with the multitude. It is therefore within society as a whole (and no longer solely in the factories) that labour extends productive networks, capable of innovating the world of commodities, putting to work the entirety of rational and affective desires of mankind. Exploitation is determined through this same extension. So much for technical composition. But we now have to ask about the political composition of the new labour power, since (characterized as it is by the embodiment of the tool: in immaterial labour the tool is the brain) it presents itself on the market in conditions of maximum mobility (which is also an exodus from the disciplinary forms of capitalist power) and in maximum flexibility – which is also political autonomy, the search for self-valorization, and the refusal of representation. How do we locate Leninism within this new condition of labour power? In short, how do we transform the exodus and self-valorization of immaterial labour into a new class struggle, into an organized desire for the appropriation of social wealth, and for the liberation of subjectivity? How can we connect this new and changed reality to the strategic project of communism? How can we renew the old within an utterly radical opening to the new, but at the same time preserve a 'return to the origins' (in this case, to Leninism) – which was Machiavelli's requirement for every true revolution?

Marx was tied to a 'manufacturing' phenomenology of industrial labour: this led to a basically self-management conception of the party and the social dictatorship of the proletariat. Lenin was bound from the start to a vanguardist perspective of the party which – before the Russian Revolution – anticipated in Russia the transition from manufacture to 'heavy industry', and then gave itself the strategic task of governing that industry. For both Marx and Lenin, the relationship between the technical composition of the proletariat and political strategy is called the 'Common' or the 'Communist Party' – and it is the 'Common' or the 'Party' that carries out the analysis of the existing situation and enacts a full circulation between (subversive) political strategy and the (bio-political) organization of the masses. The party is a motor of the production of subjectivity – or, rather, it is the tool for the production of subversive subjectivity.

Our issue is: what form should the production of subjectivity take for today's taking of power by the immaterial proletariat? Or, to put it another way: if today the context of production is that of the social cooperation of immaterial labour, which we call general intellect, then how will it be possible to construct the subversive body of general intellect, making of communist organization the lever, the point of generation of revolutionary new corporalities, the powerful base of the production of subjectivity? This brings us fully into the question of 'Lenin beyond Lenin'.

The subversive body of general intellect

At this point we have to introduce this topic, almost as a parenthesis. But, as sometimes happens in Socratic dialogue, a parenthesis may shed new light on a concept. There is, in Marx's *Grundrisse*, the famous 'Fragment on machines': in it Marx seems to construct a 'natural history' (that is, linear, continuous, necessary) of capital towards general intellect . . . general intellect is the product of capitalist development. This is an ambiguous conclusion, both for us and also – already – for Lenin (who obviously could not have read the *Grundrisse*, but who had that logic of rupture that characterizes Marxist thought, making any idea of a natural continuity of capitalist development impossible). In effect, beyond the objectivist illusion that often insinuates itself into the critique of political economy, this is also the way that things were for Marx: the development that generates general intellect is, for him, a process that is far from natural:

it is, on the one hand, full of life (the life forces – all of them – of production and reproduction, the biopolitical context of capitalist society); on the other, this process is powerfully contradictory (general intellect is not only the product of the struggles against waged labour, but also the representation of that anthropological tendency which is represented in the refusal of work: it is, in short, the result – revolutionized – of the tendential fall of the capitalist rate of profit).

In fact, here we are in an entirely biopolitical situation. It is this that joins the Marx of general intellect to Lenin and to us: it is the fact that we are all actors – women and men – of that world of production that constitutes life – that we are all the flesh of development. It is this reality of capitalist development, this new flesh of it, where the potentialities of knowledge mix inseparably with those of production, and scientific activities – in a most singular and beautiful way – intermix with passions: well, this *bios* (or rather this biopolitical reality that characterizes the industrial revolution after 1968) is what some writers and teachers (who declared themselves to be communists when the night was getting darker) choose to call 'bodies without organs', *Corps sans Organes*. I continue to call all this '*flesh*'. Perhaps it will have the strength to make itself *body* and to create for itself the full complement of organs that it requires. Perhaps: because this would take a demiurge capable of rendering the event real, i.e. an external vanguard able to turn the flesh into body. The body of General Intellect. Or perhaps, as other writers have suggested, is it possible for the becoming-body of general intellect to be determined by the word that general intellect itself articulates, so that general intellect becomes the demiurge of its own body?

I do not believe that the choice of a possible way forward can be identified by us: this is something that only a movement of struggle will be able to decide. What is certain, however, is that within the perspective of a maturing of general intellect we must anticipate experimentation. Because it is only in this way, opposing to the natural history of capital those insoluble contradictions that Marx has invented, that the genealogy of general intellect will be constituted as a subversive force. To define the body of general intellect is, in fact, the same as to assert power of the subjects that inhabit it, the violence of the crisis that shakes its ambiguity, the clash of teleologies that traverse it: and to decide on which side one stands in this chaos. If we decide that within general intellect the subject has *potenza*, because it is nomadic and independent; that here, therefore, cooperation wins over the market; that the teleology of the common prevails over that of the individual and of the private – here we would have taken the side of the body of general intellect. It is a constitution that is born from the militancy of people who are formed within immaterial and cooperative labour and who have decided to live as subversive association.

The 'biopolitics of Leninism' is thus found to be embedded here in the new contradictions of 'beyond Lenin'. With Lenin we decide to make the body of general intellect into the subject of the organization of a new life.

Spaces and temporalities

But 'beyond Lenin' is not only the recognition of a new reality and thus a renewed discovery of the urgency of organization: it must also be the spatial and temporal determination of a project for liberation. The body is always localized in space and always exists in *that specific time*. The production of subjectivity – to become effective – requires spatial and temporal determinations. In the case of Russia, which was a place and a time, there was for Lenin a single and absolute determination – here and now, or never. What are the space and the time of possible subversive organization and revolution for the immaterial, overflowing and autonomous proletariat?

Many difficulties arise from recognizing the spatial dimension of a new Leninist project. We live within Empire and we know that any revolutionary initiative that moves within limited spaces (even within very large nation-states) will have no outcome. It is clear that the only Winter Palace recognizable today is the White House! Needless to say, not so easy to attack . . . Moreover, the more imperial power strengthens itself, the more its political representation becomes complex and integrated at the global level. Although it has the USA at its apex, the Empire is not American – it is the Empire of collective capital. As for the other side, obviously there can be no space for the party that is not the International, an observation so obvious as to be almost pointless.

What is decisive for the renewal of Leninism is not so much the theoretical reaffirmation of a point where leverage must be applied in order to multiply the forces of subversion. What is interesting in 'Lenin beyond Lenin' is to identify in practical terms the point in the imperial chain where it is possible to force reality. Now, this is not, and will no longer be, a 'weak point' – rather, it will be the point at which the strongest resistance, insurrection and the hegemony of general intellect are concentrated – in short, the constituent power of the new proletariat. At the basis of the revolutionary mechanism of the production of subjectivity there is therefore, formally, the International: concretely, politically, materially, there is not a space but a place, not a horizon but a point, that on which the event is possible.

The theme of space for the party is thus subordinated to a specific *kairos*, to the untimely *potenza* of an event – it is the arrow that general intellect unleashes in order to recognize itself as body.

What needs to be said regarding the temporality of the Leninist neo-party in the age of post-Fordist globalization is in some ways analogous to what I have just said. As in the case of space, for temporality, too, the determinations have fallen. Economic history and political history are less and less definable according to rhythmic sequences; equally unrecognizable are the cyclical regularity of the epochs of exploitation or the creative periods of working-class struggle, which characterized the whole century from 1870 to 1970 . . . So what is the temporality that is entrusted to the Leninist party – today – to control, to use, to transform? Here too the indistinction is very strong: as when we talked about spatiality and places and saw how the nation-state had become a fiefdom of Empire, and the developed North and the underdeveloped South were now intertwined with each other in an identical destiny, so the temporality is indistinguishable. Only a specific *kairos* will be able to make it possible for the body of general intellect to emerge.

But what does this mean? There is no theoretical conclusion to a position formulated in such terms. Now more than ever, militancy and experimentation in this area are crucial. To us, it is clear that the Leninist mechanism of intervening at a weak point and at a critical time, objectively determined, is completely ineffective. It is clear that only when the party of immaterial labour power can present an energy which is higher than that of the forces of the capitalist exploitation – only then will a project of liberation be possible. The anti-capitalist decision only becomes effective where subjectivity is stronger, where it can construct 'civil war' against the Empire.

Dictatorship without sovereignty, or 'absolute democracy'

At this point we have to admit that our argument is not as probative as we expected at the start of our Socratic appeal. It is true that, to reaffirm the figure of the Leninist party (which watches over power and constitutes freedom within an untimeliness and absolute decision), we have established some important premises (the self-manifestation of general intellect and the possibility of giving it body; the tendential centrality of immaterial labour, exodus and nomadism; the autonomy and self-valorization which are in play in this context; and finally the contradictions that mark the relationship between globalization and the interplay of its inner mechanisms with resistance and subversion) – but, beyond that, we have to admit that we have reached no kind of conclusion. If we do not fill this framework with content, determination and singular *potenza*, entrusting ourselves to the *kairos* risks missing the essence of the matter. This appeal to *kairos* can perhaps give form to the production of subjectivity, but it is terribly exposed to tautology, when it does not propose subversive words and contents . . . We need to give content to the *kairos* of general intellect, and give food to the body of revolutionary general intellect. So what constitutes a revolutionary decision today? By what contents is it characterized?

To answer this question, we need to make a small detour. We must remember the limited nature of the Leninist point of view (which nevertheless represented a huge advance, beyond the manufacturing culture of Russian social democracy). Its revolutionary decision, in making itself constituent power, in fact concealed within itself a model of industry which was Western – American, in fact. Modern industrial development is the skeleton in the cupboard of the Bolshevik theory of revolution. The model of revolutionary management, or the project of the constituent Russians, was determined by this premise. And in the longer term it was perverted by it. Today the situation is radically altered. There is no longer a working class complaining about the lack of a management plan for industry and society, whether it be direct management or management via the state. And even if this project were to be reactivated, it could not be hegemonic over the proletariat and/or mass intellectuality; nor could it attack a capitalist power that has shifted to other levels (financial, bureaucratic, communicational . . .) of command. Thus revolutionary decision today must base itself on another constituent schema: it no longer sets as its precondition an industrial axis and/or development of the economy but, through that multitude in which mass intellectuality is configured, it will propose the programme of a liberated city in which industry is shaped to the requirements of life, society is shaped to science, and work is shaped to the multitude. Constituent decision, here, becomes a democracy of a multitude.

So we come to the conclusion of this section. Here a great radicality is demanded of the party for the transformation of the movement into the exercise of constituent power. Constituent power always anticipates the law, therefore it is always dictatorship. (But there are dictatorships and dictatorships. The Fascist one is not the same as the communist one, even if we do not prefer the latter to the former.) The fact is that political decision is always the production of subjectivity, and subjectivity is a producing of concrete bodies, of masses and/or multitudes of bodies – therefore each subjectivity is different from the others.

Today what interests to us is the subjectivity of the body of general intellect. In order to transform the world that surrounds it, it has to use force – a force that will be ordered by the constituent *potenza*. Naturally, this exercise of constituent *potenza* also may have outcomes that are either positive or negative. There is no measure to decide in advance the criterion for what the multitudes will create. However, so that things are clear and nobody can accuse us of working for some indiscriminate dictatorship, covered by hypocritical words and today more dangerous than ever, because hidden in the vulgarity of a social that is homogeneous in consumption – let us say straightaway that the dictatorship which we want, and which we believe constitutes the treasure of a re-found Lenin, may also be called 'absolute democracy'. This was the name that Spinoza gave to that form of government which the multitude exercised over itself. Spinoza had a lot of courage in adding that adjective 'absolute' to one of the equivalent forms of government which ancient theory had handed down: monarchy versus tyranny, aristocracy versus oligarchy, democracy versus anarchy. Spinoza's 'absolute democracy' separates itself from the theory of forms of government. According to this theory, it could be, and has been, covered in negative epithets. But 'absolute democracy' is, in fact, a term which is particularly suited to the invention of a new form of freedom, or rather to the production of a people in the making.

But perhaps the fundamental motivation that sustains us in this proposal of 'absolute democracy' is the knowledge that from this term is excluded (by force of the things, spaces and temporalities of postmodernity) all contamination by modernity's concept of sovereignty. We must – and we can, if we are able to grasp his biopolitical valency – carry Lenin outside of the universe of modernity (from the sovereign industrial model) in which he lived: we can translate his revolutionary decision into a new production of subjectivity – communist and autonomous – of the postmodern multitude.

12

LESSON 5

Logic and the Theory of the Inquiry: Militant Practice as Subject and Episteme

In our discussion of the historical causality and ontological genealogy of the concept of Empire, we have tried to 'subsume within the concept' (as Hegel and Marx would have put it) broad social movements and the transformations in techniques of government and in the structural workings of sovereignty. In other words, we have been doing political science. But there's more to it than that. Through this kind of analysis our intention has not only been to identify functional transitions, but also to arrive at an understanding of the shifts and contradictions contained in the way events unfold. However, our discussion thus far has left various methodological questions unresolved. So it is time to examine more deeply some of the topics raised in the previous chapters.

A first point which emerges as needing closer examination is what happens when the ontological element (the movement) meets the institutional element (politics). The relationship between social movements and institutional change goes hand in hand with transformations in the actual nature of those movements. *Fundamental* here is the shift from the hegemony of material labour to immaterial labour – in other words, we have to analyse those processes within the workforce which, as well as transforming our ways of working, have also changed people's ways of being and expressing themselves in the world. If we want to understand the logic of the historical evolution, this is where it is to be found, within these ontological dimensions of work. There would be no such thing as effective struggles if they were not framed within, tied to, produced together with this profound transformation in the world of work. Struggles arise not merely from problems of wage-share or the quantification/distribution/antagonism of the relation between wages and profits – they have always also (and above all) developed around the *intention of liberating labour*. And nowadays any liberation of work has to be addressed within a process that is leading tendentially to a hegemony of immaterial labour. The 'refusal of work' slogans ['*rifiuto del lavoro*'] of the 1960s and 1970s were positive slogans, insofar as a refusal of the Taylorist and Fordist paradigm of work went hand in hand with a desire to transform work. That desire made possible the discovery of more advanced forms of productivity of human labour, at the same time as bringing about increasingly advanced conditions, and real possibilities, of liberation from the kind of hard labour, poverty and physical destruction of people's bodies that characterized the work of the mass worker. So, moving the analysis forward, we can now identify new dimensions of work which embrace the entirety of life. If we look at this shift from a methodological point of view, we find that it gives us a way of understanding events that can delve into these processes and help us to see work not simply as productive (economic) activity, but also in terms of emotions, communication, life – in short, ontology; all those dimensions which create life and productive activity as a single interwoven entity, as one single effective reality. (*Note*: it is very important that this way of seeing things – the shift *from labour to the biopolitical* – is taken on board, because this enables us to deal with a series of central problems such as those of social reproduction and the problems that have been raised by feminism, bringing them into the frame and dealing with them in a shared context of discussion.)

Another point in need of closer examination, especially when it comes to methodology, is the *definition of the multitude*. We have defined *the multitude* not only as a class concept, related to the experience of (and transformations in) work; nor solely as a political concept, in other words as a democratic proposition geared to the construction of new relations between citizen singularities; but also as a mechanism of *potenza* extended over every aspect of life, endowed with the ability to express the common, and which has a strengthening of that *potenza* and a redefining of life, of production and of freedom. In saying this we are restating what we have said many times before – that we are in a phase of transition – a long and complex phase, of which it is hard to grasp all the possible outcomes. However, the concept of 'the multitude', as we have framed it, gives an idea of a direction in which we might be moving and helps to free ourselves increasingly from any dialectics of sublimation and synthesis (hence from the Hegelian method of *Aufhebung*). Here what the method reveals is the multitude as an ontological limit; and thus it defines itself as a method which is syncopated, interrupted, open and untimely. *Similarly to the multitude, method submits to event; it is event.*

Here we have another crucial point, one which enables us to follow the production of subjectivity in the area where it sits with, and develops, the possible convergence between the activity of work and the *construction of the 'common'*. Here our method starts from below. But building from below also means having to confront huge obstacles. In Lesson 4, in our discussion of war as the final stage of capitalist control, both the author and his readers will have experienced a certain vertigo in facing the realities of the present phase of history and in having to deal with them. But in this area, as in others, there is no way of avoiding the risks. We have to move forward, and the only way to do so is to embark on a project of research, following a logic of 'full immersion', putting ourselves right into it. We have to move always from below, in the knowledge that there is no longer an 'outside'. Now, if we want to consolidate this position the crucial point is *to define cooperation*. I said above that the model for postmodern production is linguistic cooperation – a model not only because of the material fact that machines function through languages, but also because via language there emerge ever-original forms of cooperation between individuals. And we find that we are no longer dealing with individuals, but with singularities in a condition of cooperation. But if linguistic cooperation is a productive cooperation, if everything is within this cooperation, if, within all this, the multitude is a constitutive force, then we need to ask the question: what is the articulation of diversity, of command, within these flows? For example, what is the difference between the manager and the worker, between the activities of the one and the activities of the other? Or, to put it in terms of method, how can we evaluate and, if necessary, cut through this development from within? The form of cooperation is not in itself sufficient to resolve the problem. Here probably what we need to follow is the (Marxian) thread which identifies the common as the sole dimension which can enable us to break through eventual confusions, equivocation and lack of clarity. *The common is that which distinguishes.* This is what enables us to divide the manager from the worker: in fact it is only the affirmation of the 'common' which permits us to understand the flows of production from within and to separate the (alienating) capitalist flows from the flows that are re-compositional of knowledge and freedom. The problem will thus be resolved through a break at the level of practice, one which can reaffirm the centrality of common practice.

This is the only way we can orient our research project – by refocusing on antagonistic forms and interpreting these antagonistic forms through new figures of militancy, of convergence of knowledge and action, in the process of constructing the common. One of the most important elements in methodological terms is thus *the material determination at the level of practice, the practice which breaks with a horizon that is purely critical.* Language and cooperation have to contain within them *a break at the level of practice*, an ongoing affirmation of the centrality of common practice, which means a concrete conjoining of knowledge and action within these processes.

We can also approach this from another point of view, taking the old workerist tradition of '*con-ricerca*' as an example of a form of method. In terms of practice, 'co-research' simply meant using the method of inquiry as a means of identifying the workers' levels of consciousness and awareness among workers of the processes in which they, as productive subjects, were engaged. So one would go into a factory, make contact with the workers, and, together with them, conduct an inquiry into their conditions of work; here co-research obviously involves building a description of the productive cycle and identifying each worker's function within that cycle; but at the same time it also involves assessing the levels of exploitation which each one of them undergoes. It also involves assessing the workers' capacity for reaction – in other words, their awareness of their exploitation in the system of machinery and in relation to the structure of command. Thus, as the research moves forward, co-research builds possibilities for struggle in the factory; it also defines the lines and mechanisms of cooperation outside of the factory, and so on. Obviously, we have here a hegemony and a centrality of practice within research: a praxis which makes it possible to deepen understandings of the cycle of production and exploitation, and which is heightened when it leads into resistance and agitation – in other words, when it develops struggles. In this way it is possible to *constitute an antagonistic subject*, because this is basically what we are talking about. In short, we can build on these early techniques of workerism as a starting point. Taking this as our general framework, we then have to ask ourselves: what kind of co-research can we carry out *today*, within postmodernity, within the total transformation in the nature of work and in the organization of society? Obviously this is not an easy question, and I don't claim to have the answers here; my point is simply that we need to work on developing this perspective.

So, if we examine the question of our 'inquiry' (with all its wealth of practical possibilities) from the viewpoint of how it can be carried out today, we can say that one crucial aspect is the fundamentally *biopolitical nature of the coordinates within which it operates*: in other words, what has to be made central to the 'inquiry' is *the human body*. That is, things to do with the body, with bodily life, have to be brought into play if we want to constitute, represent and begin to define constellations of any kind – in short, compositions. I think that this is a very important part of the biopolitical method that we are beginning to develop, breaking with the highly analytical methodologies that sociology has tended to use (what I call 'salami theories', the analytical slicing-up of the social body). Today we are probaby in a position to confront the corporeal – and as a primary terrain of analysis (and it is of some importance that we can do this having much faith in the *potenza* of the body).

Another important element that we need to take on board is the attempt to constitute the object by assuming, together and at every moment, and at the start negatively, neither simply sameness or difference, but always, in every case, singularity and its drive towards the 'common'. This methodological development is something really new and original. Previously people used to select out, analytically isolate and reveal *Homo economicus*, in his various aspects, aesthetic, psychological and so on. Today we are in a position to put all this together. Whereas previously we moved from the starting point of processes of determination and specificity of phenomena considered always between sameness and difference, now, in our attempts at determination, it becomes possible to skip this dichotomic duality which often blocks us, and instead conceive of *the multitude as 'common' and difference as singularity*. I think that today we have the possibility of going beyond these old dichotomies not simply in words, but in concrete terms. In singularity we enrich the contents of differences, and in the 'common' we are able to play them together, as if on a new horizon of activity. So, the central perspective around which we move is the 'common' – in other words bodies, the logical categories of singularity, and how they can be related to the 'common', and then the 'common' as an ontological premise. I also think that sociology should adopt this way of working, continually focusing on the conditions of 'common-ness' between which singularity instals itself. This is another fundamental element if we are hoping to build something. These are constellations which in some senses correspond to the layout of elements of class in the old 'composition', but here they are newly composed within the richness of a bodily common. (*Note*: we now move entirely – now that we have identified the biopolitical as our horizon of research – in contact with bodies. *Every singularity is defined as corporeal.* But biopolitical corporeality is not only biological corporeality; it is more a social corporeality. For example, when I look at the growing *precarious nature of work*, we are studying on the one hand the wearisome physicality of the life of the precarious worker in conditions of mobility and flexibility of work, but we also have to include the perception of the *potenza* of the new labour power. In other words, on the one hand we have the terrible conditions in which precarious workers are forced to work, but on the other hand we have their new quality. Thus we are able to grasp the full meaning of precariousness, moving continuously between sameness and difference and understanding the common as the basis of exploitation and, at the same time, as an activity of resistance.)

Then, taking this as our starting point, we have the transition in terms of practice, the practical option: *the rediscovery of antagonism*. But where exactly does this transition take place, wherein lies the choice of antagonism? One theoretical proposition which seems to follow from what I am saying is that we identify exploitation as command over and within the expropriation of cooperation, in other words within the possibility of blocking the activity of the multitude. Exploitation, thus, inserts itself precisely within the richness of the common and into the productivity of the multitude, and attempts to block its expression, to render it dumb, to strip the flesh from it, to distance it and to disappropriate it. By now we have to concede to alienation a powerful materiality, which affects all aspects of the body – it is an expropriation, an un-fleshing which moves against the singularity, against the 'common', and which obviously comes into conflict with the practice which is bubbling up from the expression of the 'common' and from the processes of its construction. In my view, highlighting the singular and common configuration of the new subjects of production and of the exploitation which is increasingly being visited on them, and which comes about from within these things that are dancing and moving before us in postmodernity, is the only way in which we can begin to effect a strong resonance of tone in research.

This now brings us to the final question – and this one, too, is an extremely open question. What is it that we want? Obviously we want democracy. Democracy at a global level. Democracy for all. The term 'democracy' is not the handiest of terms, but it's the only one we have. The problem is that every time we say that we want democracy, it's like putting ourselves into a trap, because people immediately ask us: 'But what exactly is it that you want? Give us a list of the democratic demands that you want implemented.' I don't think that we ought to be making lists, but rather, working on the basis of what I have said above, to draw up a schema of what exactly is *the desire for democracy*, or, better, *for the 'common'*, a methodological yardstick by which we can evaluate the various alternative propositions which are continuously coming up. Sometimes I have the impression that a whole series of proposals which, until relatively recently, would have seemed entirely utopian are today beginning to appear as increasingly realistic. There seems to be a growing awareness that we have entered into a new era. So perhaps we should draw up something similar to the *cahiers de doléances* of the period preceding the French Revolution: documents which, on the one hand, presented the Third

Estate's complaints, but which, in addition to being protests and denunciations of injustices, were also proposals for solutions. *Our method which acts from below now passes through critique in order to give a practical reply to that critique.*

The problem we need to address is, how can one today conceive of democracy at a global level? An initial critical approach (of the kind that we have practised in *Empire*) has documented the development of Empire's mechanisms of control, division and hierarchization. We have seen, furthermore, how these mechanisms of control are implemented and come to be exercised through a continuous action of war. Thus *the real problem is how to help to develop the subversive desire for the 'common' which is currently being expressed in the multitude, balancing it against war, institutionalizing it, and transforming it into constituent potenza.*

In the preceding lessons I suggested that we have at least three elements capable of configuring the definition of the multitude in terms of the 'common'. The *first* element is that of social ontology, in other words the proposition that immaterial labour does not require command and that one aspect of immaterial and intellectual labour is the capacity to create *excess*. An excess which is developed via 'networks'. Thus, as regards the ontology of labour, we have to address the problem of how to guarantee forms of 'networking' in any future democracy. The 'network' is a communicational network in which cooperative values are formed – in the full meaning of the term, both productive and political.

The *second* element is that of the 'common', in other words the material reality of a production which nowadays needs neither capital nor exploitation in order to exist. Seen from this point of view, of the *the accumulation of the 'common', capitalism is becoming ever-increasingly parasitical.* Here the common is what permits the constitution of being. And this 'common' cannot be reappropriated by anyone or privatized by anyone. So on the one hand we have the theories of labour showing the inefficacy of command, while on the other the theories of the social reveal the inalienable nature of the 'common'. This 'common' is the inalienable material on which we can build democracy.

The *third* element configuring the process of the multitude is that of freedom [*libertà*]. Without freedom there is no creative work. *Without freedom there is neither cooperation nor the common.*

Having brought these three elements into the frame we now need to shift to an examination of conceptions of rights and democracy, both juridical and bourgeois. In this sense I would say that *Marx's writings on rights* are still valid, and particularly his critique of Hegel's theory of right. Naturally, this critique must be extended to the democratic rights existing in our own time, in which formal equality is matched by the reality of substantial inequality.

All this becomes very important when we move to consider the new terrains of world-wide constitution and of a global system of law. It is important to stress that the development of capitalism tends to render ineffective any regulatory action on the part of the nation-state. In modernity, the development of capitalism took place through the state, but nowadays, within postmodernity, capitalism has reappropriated the whole fabric of society, at the multinational level, except that then it resorts to interventions by the nation-state in case of necessity. It is clear that when we speak of common property, when we talk about work organized in 'networks', and of guarantees of freedom on this terrain, we have to deal with the question of globalization. Dealing with globalization is crucial, because it enables us to be very clear that we are beyond any guarantee on the part of the nation-state, and beyond any illusion of a return to the equilibrium of the nation-state. Today democracy has to be built in the relationships between the multitudes, and thus it constructs new social relations and new law. Here I am not talking about the destruction of right, but of new juridical forms that will be capable of establishing norms in line with the three principles outlined above. Furthermore, there need to be sanctions against those who wish to re-establish command, against those seeking to introduce criteria of ownership or control over the 'network', and against anyone seeking to block access to it or control its nodes. There must be sanctions against anyone inventing technological and/or juridical–political instruments in order to block the circulation of knowledge and this huge area of 'commonness' which can give nourishment to both production and life.

At this point you may object that I have not talked about logic. Or perhaps you will concede that I have addressed it in allusive terms, in my discussion of the inquiry and the theory of co-research, and the practical activities which can and must be developed in the area of social knowledge. But this is not so. In all the above I really have been talking about logic. It is only because I have not discussed it in academic terms that the theme of logic appears to be missing – but, I repeat, that is not the case. So, to explain myself better, also in academic terms, and to show that militants also have no difficulty in traversing our regions of rhetoric, what follows is a schema, or rather a 'high' filter, of what I have outlined thus far in terms of logic. In fact it is a schematic resumé of the lesson, but with the addition of some bibliographical references.

1   *The preamble to the discussion of logic as* theory of inquiry *is to be found in Marx's* Einleitung *(as we have seen previously). I would also refer the reader to* John Dewey, Logic: The Theory of Inquiry *(Holt, Rinehart and Winston, New York, 1938). In Alan Ryan's* John Dewey *(Harvard University Press, Cambridge, MA, 2001), the author shows the extent to which the lines of American empirical logic cross with the lines of Marxian logic. Thus the thinking of Rodolfo Mondolfo and of Sydney Hook are of our time. In substance, what we have here is praxis being taken as a central element of epistemology and politics. But more than that, in my introduction here I also stressed the relationship between language, rhetoric, dialogue and invention, and the ways in which they interweave in two dimensions that we find congenial: on the one hand the Spinozan logic of the common name, and on the other the rediscovery of the common name in postmodern logic (for this see my* Kairos, Alma Venus, Multitudo*).*

2   The inquiry as a procedure related to logic. *What does this mean? It means that here, in our effort to create a logic of research, we have consistently developed a process of thinking which moves from the* 'constitution of the object' *(the inquiry) to the dialogic explication of the constitution of the object (co-research), and then to the definition of the constitutive subject. Thus we have a kind of* return from the object to the subject. *This has always been the progress of a logic that is revolutionary, as Ryan explains in his book* John Dewey, *and, if we simplify things, in the US in the 1920s and 1930s the transition from revolutionary liberalism to the New Deal. But, mutatis mutandis, this* 'return from the object to the subject' *could also be seen as part of every revolutionary experience. In the earlier lessons I showed how the logic of the subject lived between causality and discontinuity of development.*

The identification of the logic of the event is the central point of our discussion. Thus we can say that the 'common name' (concept) always oscillates between sameness and difference, but is determined between singularity and the common. But if this is true, it follows that the subject is given within a process of production of subjectivity, and thus as production of determined temporalities and spatialities. But at the same time as we have seen the subject being formed in the production of the common (that is, through cooperation), at that same moment we show how the purely logical dimension is inadequate for the full completion of the inquiry. Cooperation in itself does not explain antagonism; therefore we have to take antagonism as our starting point.

*3   Inquiry as an ethical–political procedure. In the Fordist society of the mass worker, the inquiry as an ethical-political way of working was carried out under the label of co-research [*con-ricerca*]. In co-research the epistemological procedure and that of militancy/agitation were closely linked. See G. Borio, F. Pozzi, G. Roggero,* Futuro anteriore. Dai 'Quaderni Rossi' ai movimenti globali, *DeriveApprodi, Rome, 2002. When we speak of the inquiry as an ethical–political* dispositif, *we are not, of course, avoiding the more decisively cognitive and generally epistemological problems – far from it; in fact they are brought into the frame and deployed within a process of collective learning. The inquiry as an ethical–political mechanism is always, in some sense, a* Bildungsroman. *The question of the formation of elites is interwoven with that of the centrality of praxis, and the process of the formation of elites is closely tied to that of the organization of the antagonism. Clearly here a series of other problems opens up, accentuated in particular by the changing historical context and by class composition. What does inquiry, as an ethical–political mechanism mean* within postmodern society – *hence an inquiry no longer in the Fordist realities of the mass worker, but among the precariat, in a situation of mobility and flexibility of labour, in a context of immateriality of the work done and the hegemony of cooperation? I don't think that the answer is much different from that which applied in the case of co-research – I mean in terms of method and of the constitutive progression of the subject. In my own case, I was involved in this kind of work in the 1990s, in the journal* Futur antérieur, *published in Paris by Harmattan, to which I refer the reader. For the question of how co-research can be carried out within postmodernity and in a situation of cooperation among immaterial labour, see A. Negri et al.,* Des entreprises pas comme les autres

[Enterprises unlike Others], Publisud, Paris 1993; and A. Negri et al., Le bassin du travail immatériel *[The Pool of Immaterial Work],* L'Harmattan, Paris 1996.

4   Inquiry and the logic of language. *Once we have established that there is a relationship between inquiry as a linguistic mechanism and the new realities of production in postmodernity, where language is a fundamental means of production and productive cooperation, we have to redefine the inquiry in terms of the logic of language. Paolo Virno, both in* Grammatica della moltitudine *[Grammar of the Multi-tude: For an Analysis of Contemporary Forms of Life, Semiotexte, Los Angeles, 2004] and in* Il ricordo del presente. Saggio sul tempo storico *(Bollati Boringhieri, Turin, 1999), has created many openings in this area. For myself, as well as drawing on Virno's examination of the problem of language as a productive force (productive of cooperation and singularity), I draw on the works of Bakhtin, where the linguistic constitution of the real is connotated in materialistic terms that are very strong.*

Once we pursue this kind of method it is clear that it brings us, once again, up against some of the great issues of communism. This means that our method is well matched to the *epochal alternative* which we are living, in which the *crisis of neo-liberalism* has, as its alternative, the *objectives of communism*: the reappropriation of the factories, the egalitarian distribution of wealth, the collective development of knowledge and so on. For years and years, ever since the great post-1968 crisis, nobody has dared to talk about these things. Today we are beginning to talk about them again, and to adopt the method which leads us to this possibility of expression, because we know that we live on the threshold of a terminal crisis: either the restoration of a very harsh past, or the hope for a new world. Here we have to decide – *and it is around the problem of decision that politics is born.*

However, before offering a few notes about the problem of decision, it would be useful to reflect on this point and think that, in this terrible and bloody period of transition which we have now fully entered, in a sense everything is possible. Imagination and decision must, therefore, be part and parcel of the movement of the multitude, in the desire of expression that the multitude produces. Within this imagination, *democratic representation*, which has always been offered to us as a fundamental element that guarantees our liberty, is, to say the least, a monstrous mystification. The problem currently posed by the imagination of the multitude is that of *combining sovereign power [potenza] and the productive capacity of subjects.* Our whole discussion of the biopolitical as we have developed it thus far, leads us towards this conclusion. But how can we set about organizing this desire of the multitude? How can we set about organizing another democracy? Nowadays, at the national level, democracy no longer exists. At the world level, democracy is completely unthinkable. And yet it is these unthinkable things which today constitute the actuality of desire . . . We have to begin to talk in Enlightenment terms, thinking up new electoral colleges at world level which no longer correspond to nation-states but can traverse the face of the world, redressing the balance between rich and poor zones, between whites and blacks, between yellows and greens and so on . . . creating hybrids and thus overturning political confines and limits, putting our energies into the construction of the common. Constitutional imagination, this is what we need . . . Enlightenment thinking, this is what is necessary . . .

But let us return to decision. What does it mean to pose the problem of the relationship between the common experience of the multitude and the ethical–political (and also juridical) concept of decision? I think that we need to talk about all this, in this and in many other places, but the eventual answer can only be given at the level of the language of the movement – *within the movement.* And, anyway, it is within the movements that these issues are reaching maturity: the parties are dead and buried, and now it is the movements which pose the problems and hint at their solutions. Now, as far as the problem of the decision of the multitude is concerned, there is something which has been evident in these movements, from Seattle to the present time: namely, that people are no longer talking about taking power, but about *doing power,* about making another kind of power, and while we all know that this is utopianism, we also know that it is rendered necessary and realistic by the dizzying realities of the epochal transition that we are living through. We cannot wait for two or three hundred years for the decision of the multitude to become real!

But this might always turn out to be the case – defeat might be inevitable . . . In that case, let us pull out! To the radicality of constituent power there exists the alternative possibility of exodus, an exodus which is itself constructive, which expresses positive forms of the relationship between decision and the multitude, and therefore between freedom and the production of the common. If we find that we cannot construct another form of power, then the multitude can declare a strike, a desertion, removing itself from power . . . And these processes, *between constituent power and exodus*, interweave and alternate with each other. They are like waves, these decisions of the multitude, following one upon the other; they are terms that are damnably hard and strong, produced by a stormy sea: there is no longer a grinding down to be endured by the masses at the hands of power; on the contrary, there is an ontological insurrection of the multitude. We are living the biopolitical.

13

Following in Marx's Footsteps

Michael Hardt and Antonio Negri

But, in general, the protective system of our day is conservative, while the free trade system is destructive. It breaks up
old nationalities and pushes the antagonism of the proletariat and the bourgeoisie to the extreme point. In a word,
the free trade system hastens the social revolution. It is
in this revolutionary sense alone, gentlemen, that I vote in
favour of free trade.

K. Marx, 9 January 1848

Production thus not only creates an object for the subject
but also a subject for the object.

K. Marx, Grundrisse, trans. Martin Nicolaus,
Penguin Books, London, 1993, p. 92

Five points regarding method in transformation

In his *Einleitung* [the Introduction to the *Grundrisse*] of 1857,
Marx sets out a method which is consubstantial with the object
which his research addresses: both the method and the substance,
both the form and the content, work together and change together.
The method of 1857 is the method of historical materialism,

which has as its object of examination the formation of capitalism and the socio-political conditions brought about by its development. The method advanced in the *Einleitung* was perfectly matched to its object, and it made a major contribution to revolutionary thinking throughout the twentieth century. Today, however, we need a new *Einleitung*, because the essence of capitalism (its maturity and its global stabilization) has changed radically. We need to address the question of whether there is an expositional coherence, *when this coherence is defined as a matching between the method and the construction of the common names that it produces*. There is nothing of the dialectical in this assumption: whereas Marx, in revealing the correspondence between method and matter in his research, and then in offering its conceptual exposition, developed a *dispositif* which was dialectical, we do not believe that this redundancy of metaphysical premises is necessary to our *Darstellung*. The givenness of the event, the causal concatenation, the definition of common names is given, in fact, on the surface of the real.

As we have said, Marx in his *Einleitung* proceeds through an articulated definition of the methodological instance. For him the first elements of the method of the critique of political economy consist in (a) *determinate abstraction*; (b) the definition of the *tendency*; (c) the assumption of the *practical criterion* of verification of the true name; and finally (d) the construction, based on all these elements, of a method of *déplacement* and of consequent *constitution* of an object which is *spurious*, in the sense that the subject acts within it. Thus between (c) and (d) is formed the principle of *antagonism*. Marx's methodology is, therefore, a methodology which takes as its starting point a powerful abstraction and then descends to praxis and subjectivity, in order then to rise again to revolutionary displacement and the conscious constitution of alterity: this is the same process as the process of liberation, but here embodied in epistemology.

In *Empire* we developed some methodological outlines which we shall compare here with those of Marx. In the first place, we tried to define how *historical causality* operated in the era of postmodernity. The problem was that it was no longer possible to start from determinate abstraction, i.e. from the formation of the concept as an independent, scientific, independent activity; rather, we had to move within a pervasive historical experience and gauge our positions against that continuous turmoil (consisting of causes and repercussions, not of effects but, precisely, of events and unexpected emergences) which characterizes *the historical styles of postmodernity*. Thus historical causality was what was determined by movements and struggles, but this determining, far from indicating an abstract direction or a general final result, broke them up and presented itself as a process of fragmentation. Thus we have strong causality and no teleology, temporal continuities and discontinuities, untimely actions of subjectivity and the constitution of new subjects: through all these transitions the causal mechanism rearticulated itself into *free-moving dispositifs* and determinism dissolved across a wide horizon of *constitutive acts having a powerful subjective imprint*.

When we move from historical method to social ontology, the discontinuities and *potenze* of the real become still more obvious. Inasmuch as immaterial labour (intellectual, affective, relational and so on) becomes hegemonic over material labour, social ontology itself presents itself under a different form, since the product of intellect is always excedent; and, to this *excedence* of immateriality (what we refer to as invention-power) is added an excedence of *cooperation*, in which the common of the multitude is deployed among singularities. In this way *social ontology becomes biopolitical*. This means that the production process invests life itself, where by production process we mean the complex of knowledge and passions, of languages and emotions, that make up subjectivity. The first point of our methodological inquiry, the one defined by the non-teleological causality of the political and social movements, thus stressed the necessity of immersing method within the historical process; in the second moment, that of social ontology, *method* finds itself, on the contrary, *strongly reactivated by the excedence* which immateriality offers in the immanence of the process, and thus by the biopolitical pulsation of the process itself. From this point of view, the level of immanence breathes.

This brings us to our third point: as a consequence of all the above, causality and excedence of knowledge, history and bio-politics, intersecting at the level of a powerful immanence, have to *express themselves*. This is the moment at which the descent of method into the real becomes most evident. Causality overflows the margin of the event, and method itself becomes constituent.

Here the multitude has to confront the driving force internal to the discovery of the common, must test itself against the constitution of a *telos*. Here, unlike what we have in Marx's *Einleitung*, method is not a dialectical to-and-fro, and does not need to bring transcendence into method in order to illustrate the transformations of reality. Here method enjoys the absolute immanence of *being within* a historical process that produces itself as a continuous deepening *towards* and *within* subjectivity. The method has not proceeded (as is the case in Marx) from abstraction to subjectivity and to constitution, but has brought constitution back *within the historical flow*. Immanence has no need to pretend transcendence, not even in instrumental terms: here the dialectics really has been extinguished.

It now remains to illustrate a fourth moment of the method. This point is not so important for the general configuration of the method, but is important inasmuch as it directs our attention to the question of singularity (which can very well be our own, both specific and determined) . . . of the singularity which drives the method forward and forms it as methodological action. *The production of subjectivity* that we have grasped as a general *dispositif* of method is here turned into (and confronts itself with) the *production of self*. There is no substantial distinction, but a huge prominence given to passion, to specific corporeality, to each person's singular history . . . As Foucault says: 'We believed ourselves to be moving away and we find ourselves again on the vertical of ourselves. The journey rejuvenates things and ages the relation to oneself' (M. Foucault, in *Le débat*, 1983, 4, 1364). When we say that the bearer of scientific method is *the militant*, a figure who 'religiously' ties the creative capacity of intellect to the historical process and the biopolitical *potenza* of the possible to the constitution of a *telos* of freedom, we say that production of self cannot be conceived of except as production of the world. There is obviously something of the religious in this, but only if we talk of a religion which is completely immanent, in which revolutionizing the world is – first and foremost – a production of ourselves.

There is now a fifth point to consider. This concerns, not method in its living figures, but its formalization. After having absorbed within the method the genealogy of the historical transformation of modes of production; after having highlighted, from this perspective, the coincidence of political transformation and ontological transformation, and thus the very close relationship which links *the excedence of knowledge* (or of *living labour in its cognitive form*) to the wealth of vital development; after having excavated the constituent *potenza* of the subject within this process and, consequently but not subordinately, having highlighted the position of the singular subject in the process of production of subjectivity – given all this, let us now allow method to open onto the vertiginous heights of the postmodern transition through which we are now passing. We say: *logic as theory of inquiry*, logic as the multitude's *co-research* into itself, or rather, logic as *epistemological praxis of the multitude* . . . In this way we seek to bring logic into the real, to make decisions among subjects, to construct within the movements.

Isomorphism and genealogy

Here we would like to insert a brief parenthesis, to set out what are the differences and what are the continuities established, in this context (both methodological and ontological), in relation to the formal presuppositions of Marx's *Einleitung*. So, taking things from the viewpoint of research, let us try to understand how a series of elements in the description of the real (which, as we have seen before, particularly in Lesson 1, are given in the form of the *network*) might reproduce themselves in the same ideal form; how, in this case, there can be an *isomorphism* of networks in the real and in the ideal world. So we can take the *network* as a structure and ask ourselves: is it because our brains are structured in networks that they perceive things in this same form? Or do the various networked aspects of our social reality come into being by way of conforming to the characteristics of the network? Both hypotheses might be true. The power of the network and the network war modify social reality and at the same time correspond to new conditions and modalities of thought. We should not view the history of ideas or forms of thought as a linear historical progression. In fact, profound changes are taking place in models of thinking, which radically reconfigure the customary categories of knowledge (what is defined as normal or abnormal, clear or obscure), and also determine the limits between the thinkable and the unthinkable. These ruptures or modifications of epistemic regimes, through which we think, are analogous to reforms taking place in other social arenas: in public institutions, political groups, economic activities, cultural practices, and so on.

In other words, what we see in the proliferation of networks is an example of the general phenomenon of formal correspondence between changes in our social reality and changes in our ways of thinking. By this we mean that, first of all, every thought belongs to a specific socio-historical context, as if it were imprinted by it; and, secondly (and even more importantly), the different domains of thought and the various elements of social reality are isomorphic and they are modified isomorphically. Let us now consider what might be the most effective counter-example to Descartes' famous hypothesis 'I think, therefore I am', a foundational method which seeks the truth of an individual mind which is independent from the body and from its physical world. Descartes was able to conceive of himself as having no body, and that there was no world or place in which to manifest himself, and that only his thinking was certain proof of his own existence. So it might appear disconcerting when, in that same piece of writing, Descartes locates his revelation of the world in a specific place. 'I was then in Germany, to which country I had been attracted by the wars which are not yet at an end.' Descartes arrives at his discovery on a day in 1616, probably 10 November, when, as a soldier in the Thirty Years War, he is obliged to winter in a room heated by a single stove. What have the war, and Descartes' role in it, to do with an eternal truth such as 'I think, therefore I am'? Why does Descartes bother to inform us about his temporal and spatial circumstances? It is not hard to see how the devastating realities of an insane and hopeless war might have led a person to stop 'studying the book of the world' and make himself the object of study instead. I can imagine that this horrible world does not exist, and that my thinking self is the only clear and certain reality. But it would be extremely reductive to conceive of Descartes' methodological discovery as merely the reaction of a distraught soldier at war. That would establish too narrow, mechanical and linear a relation between cause and effect. On the contrary, we have to historicize Descartes' discovery within a wider frame. The greatness of Descartes is to have recognized a form and mode of thought that corresponded to an entire era, which was in the process of emerging. The sovereign, individual thinking self that

Descartes discovers has the same form as a variety of other figures, bound to spring up more or less contemporaneously at the dawn of modern Europe, including that of the sovereign state. Neither the Thirty Years War nor any other historical event 'caused' Descartes' discovery. Rather, the entire set of relations that constituted the reality of his situation made his theory thinkable. In more general terms, we hypothesize that every socio-historical period is distinguished by one or more isomorphisms: common structures that emerge simultaneously in various social spheres. This is what Michel Foucault alludes to, for example, when he examines the spatial distribution – the architecture – of the various social institutions of the age of modernity. Why, he asks, is the prison similar to the factory, which in turn is similar to the school, and the school to the barracks and the hospital, and so on? Foucault has used the term 'diagram' to indicate this kind of common configuration, which makes manifest affinities not only between institutional architectures, but also between schemas of thought and social practice. The diagram of our own age, the age of Empire, is the network.

But this is, precisely, a network that reveals ontological relations that may be isomorphic but not deterministic. When we bear in mind what we have mentioned previously, namely the untimeliness of causal relations (we shall return to this later), we shall also have to stress that these relations, as well as being, so to speak, *aleatory* in a downward sense in their genealogy, can be *metamorphic* in an upward sense, in their subjective projection or, simply, in their common happening.

The *Einleitung* in the conditions of postmodernity

Staying with the identification of differences and continuities with Marx's methodology, here we insert a second parenthesis.

As we know, the method of historical materialism was articulated around two points. The first was the relationship between the material, economic and social *structure* and the ideological, ideal and spiritual *superstructure*. There was a *vertical axis* that joined, in a twofold relationship of production and mystification, the real world and its image. Now, in the ontological context, the relationship between structure and superstructure merges on a flat terrain. Structure and superstructure are no longer given as separate on a vertical axis: rather, they constitute a reciprocal involvement, and this is revealed by the continuous exchange between the political and the economic (*the superstructure is*, so to speak, *put to work*). The involvement of structure and superstructure is, for example, confirmed by the increasingly intimate correspondence that we find between the concept and structure of capital and the concept and structure of sovereignty (as we have seen above, in the appendix to Lesson 1, where we discussed transformations of sovereignty).

The second point of the methodological articulation of historical materialism consisted (a transformation which we have already highlighted) in presupposing *a horizontal axis* of development, qualified by a *causal process* which is determinate and *also determinist*. This methodological parameter also becomes radically modified: in particular, today causality can be seen increasingly as an *untimely sequence* which, setting aside deterministic mechanicism, can be interpreted only in the relation between objective *dispositifs* and constitutive acts of subjects. When one says, for example, that struggles precede and determine capitalist development, a material *dispositif* is proposed (at the level of quantities and masses) to which there corresponds a series of (qualitative and innovative) constitutive acts produced by social subjects.

Having assumed the transformation of the two axes (vertical and horizontal) of the method of historical materialism, one can then, with some efficacy, elaborate 'techniques of periodization' and introduce 'definitions of periods' that reflect these modifications (as we have seen above, in the discussion of 'isomorphism and genealogy'). The transition from Fordism to post-Fordism, from modernity to postmodernity, for example, seems to represent a typical case for methodological innovation: here not only is the superstructure set to work, but, as a fundamental element of development, there appears an untimeliness which is a material figuration of the capacity of living (immaterial) labour to present itself as excedence.

Now, in this new methodological *Marx beyond Marx*, other consequences present themselves once the method has been established, as we have done, at the level of the actual experience of labour and its exploitation; in other words, once one assumes the ontological context as the exclusive point of reference.

The first consequence relates to the *law of value*. As is known and as we have repeated to the point of tedium, this can no longer be maintained in the form in which it has come down to us from Smith, via Ricardo and Marx. The temporal unit of labour as the basis for measuring the creation of value is by now a *nonsense*. Having said this, however, *labour still remains the fundamental and sole element of value creation*. But what labour are we talking about? And what labour time? This is a labour and a time which, finding a reference in the onto-logical dimension, expand on the biopolitical horizon. It is in this way that, in the ontological context, the law of value is given back to us, no longer as measure but as temporally co-extensive with the production of life, as a prospective deter-mination of living labour. It is on this terrain that, in turning from materiality to immateriality, from the intelligence of the productive act to its linguistic expression, and by constituting itself as general intellect, the law of value reveals itself in its greatest expansion.

In one final respect we have a change, and a deepening in the ontological context of the *beyond Marx*, in another characteristic of materialist method in the critique of political economy. This is *the transcendence of the dimension of economism*, in whatever form it may present itself. Quite to the contrary, our method acts in the *biopolitical*, where production manifests itself as the productive expression of the common. It will be precisely here that *exploita-tion openly reveals itself as the destruction of the common and the expropriation of cooperation*.

Thus, when we set the new form of the law of the value along-side the experience of exploitation, as our lives experience it in the present day, we can identify the parameters of the new figure of *the law of surplus value*. As regards the law of value, the students of Marx (in particular those who were dealing with the *Grundrisse* after Rosdolsky) have already shown that this could have a sig-nificance that went beyond the tautology of economic statistics only when it was interpreted as a law of exploitation, in other words as a law that showed the splitting of labour and thus its violent alienation. The same can and must be said of the way in which we read exploitation today. *Post-Fordism and postmodernity have produced the exploitation of the common: this is the new form of the law of surplus value.*

From this perspective it will be necessary to take another step: in these new conditions we need to grasp, within the path that we have followed, that *experience of antagonism*, which in Marx was closely tied to the definition of method. Determinate abstraction, tendency, a practical criterion of ascertaining truth, and finally the problematic shift and the constitution of a new ontological schema – all this lives in Marx on the basis of one essential presupposition: namely the presupposition of *crisis*, and therefore of *antagonism*, as the driving motor of the system. For Marx, moreover, to say antagonism is to say *exploitation* and *division of labour*. Antagonism and exploitation are (so to speak) homonyms (albeit in the absolute opposition which they contain), whereas exploitation and division of labour are (so to speak) synonyms, because they represent movements that converge both in concept and in reality. We therefore need to understand what is meant by *biopolitical exploitation* and the *division of labour in biopower*: this in order to maintain, *mutatis mutandis*, the political impact of Marxist analysis, albeit within this massive upheaval in the historical picture. This is how the new *Einleitung* will have to be developed in the conditions of postmodernity.

The exploitation of cooperation

What exploitation has become today is a question that is both interesting and urgent: *the problem of exploitation* is put in a new way. Marx in his time told us that there was no definition of exploitation without a critical understanding of the same, and therefore without a theory of value. The theory of value (in the Marxian sense) is a theory that institutes labour as the *substance* of the value of production and which, at the same time, fixes the *measure* of value in the intensity (the time) of exploitation of the workforce. Now, we have some reservations concerning Marx's theory of value (and we express them here, both above and in what follows), but we certainly cannot deny that the *experience of exploitation* exists: in other words, that there are workers – or simply women, men and children – who are exploited by other subjects (called 'capitalists', or '*rentiers*', or simply 'bosses'), who accumulate wealth by means of exploitation. The problem of the theory of value is therefore raised directly by the experience of exploitation we continue to suffer. However, compared with the experience that Marx had of exploitation, many things – too many, as experience tells us – have changed. This is the reason why a new theoretical perspective on value needs to be built. So, let us ask what the biggest change has been.

The first thing needing to be stressed is the new experience of *labour as activity*, that is, as a constitutive and cooperating *dispositif*. Here something very important has changed: whereas in the Bible's Genesis and throughout the entire history that precedes our times labour was seen as hard work and humanity's burden (and of the act of giving birth as pain), today we can begin to speak of the labour of all as activity and expression (and the act of giving birth as joy). This means, therefore, that we can no longer speak of labour as a quantity, as a repetition, as a simple alienation, in short as a physical entity. Of course, a person's working activity is quantifiable, it may be of greater or lesser intensity, and it is measurable (and, to this extent, alienated), but it can no longer be simplified to the point of being reduced to a temporal quantity (and to a fixed relationship between activity and time), and thus to a dimension of pure alienation. To put it another way, the labour that produces value is *first* creative activity, and *afterwards* it may be measured and/or alienated. Consequently, real (or 'complex') labour can no longer be considered as an assemblage of quotas of 'simple labour', but rather as a concatenation of creative activities, in other words as productive *cooperation*. Productive cooperation, today, invests labour, in the sense that on the one hand it makes possible its expression, and on the other it extends its effectiveness. Thus deconstructing Marx's theory of value will mean showing that the creative activity of labour and its tendency to cooperation constitute, in postmodernity, through and beyond the post-Fordist revolution, the *potenza* of living labour.

Let us stress this point. What is value within postmodern production? In this chapter of post-Marxian critique of political economy, we assume not only that value is constructed within social production (which is obvious), but also that *social production* today presents itself in a manner which *increasingly has the quality of the common*, in other words as a multiplicity of increasingly cooperative activities within the process of production (which is not so obvious). Thus a central category in the analysis of contemporary society is *cooperation*, in other words the pooling of the productive powers of a multiplicity of subjects. This pooling multiplies those energies, and in the light of this premise we shall be able to renew Marx's analysis of the commodity form, of value-creation, of money, of the social working day and so on. This means that *cooperation* is no longer imposed *from outside* the workforce, hence imposed on the workforce by the individual company or by collective capital: *it is a new force implicit in today's living labour.* As we shall see below, collective capital will try to segment and hierarchize this cooperation, which has been developed independently by material and immaterial labour, and will try to fix a new division of labour matched to the new conditions of production. But now we must stress the fact that cooperation represents the characterizing (and value-creating) face of the labour process and of the production process. And we also stress that the cooperation of living labour is, so to speak, produced and nourished by the excedence of labour as activity and expression: that is, by that excess which activity (particularly immaterial activity, the expression of the brain) always produces and which, removing itself by definition from routine and repetition, invents new forms of living and new products of life. If this is the postmodern nature of living labour and if these are the conditions of the valorization of the activity of the worker, how are we then to define *exploitation?* It absolutely has to consist in *the expropriation by capital of the expressive surplus and of the cooperation of living labour.*

The common as a 'fundamental' of the economy

Another parenthesis: in order to define cooperation as the form of labour of the multitude, two further points need to be made.

The first has to do with the set of phenomena that are more and more frequently referred to as '*external economies*' (and are accounted for as such in 'transaction cost theory'). The basis of these theories is the recognition that the production of value increasingly comes about through the capture of productive elements and of social wealth which stand *outside* the direct process of production process as such. The productivity of economic systems is here recognized as arising out of the degree of innovation (deriving from the *power* of the underlying educational, scientific and suchlike networks) and from the intensity of cooperation (deriving from the concatenation of social relations, social taxonomies and so on). So this is what 'external economies' are, common and transitive: they give social consistency to production and, through the absorption of social cooperation and of institutionality into economic life, they produce increasing outcomes; it is a raw material which is not consumed but grows still further in production: the totality of social cooperation. In fact, if one considers the revolution in production since the mid-twentieth century, one sees that, under the aegis of the common, there has been a total transformation of all the economic determinants. The basics of the economy have become social and institutional. What forms the basis of the ontology of production and the reproduction of life is the common.

Our second note is to say that the new organization of labour, and the new mode of production itself, have as their basis the most common thing in human life: *language*. Language, in this instance, is, so to speak, the model – more rarefied and yet more intense – of the external economy. And, just as happens with external economies, the linguistic common will be continuously reproduced and enriched by living labour. There is nothing abstract about this process, nothing that falls outside the logic of production; in fact one is *within*, and at the most significant point of, the new information technologies and the application of the engineering of the mind.

Now, having established that external economies and language are the raw material of productive cooperation, we can introduce another factor and elucidate this common of the external economies and of language as something which exists *before* any economic value measured by capital, as that which is the *condition* of every production, as a common heritage. So here we arrive at a fundamental conclusion of the points raised thus far: *The 'external economies' of capitalist development have to be rendered common*, which means that one must recognize the common value in culture, civilization, knowledge, professional abilities and all the ecological, associative and urban conditions that preconstitute the conditions of the capitalist economy. Now, capitalists no longer pay for these preconditions, indeed they make the public pay for them. Nevertheless, they are common, they are the living projection of labour, just as it was expressed by the multitudes of workers in the past centuries and always renewed by living labour. Often this common heritage has been consumed in external wars and in the inner destructions which followed on those wars. Often this common heritage has been used in order to construct monuments to the majesty of power, producing magnificent and shameless exaltations of authority and divinity. The paradox consists in the fact that only the living labour of the multitude can use, or rather render operational and present, this mass of past labour. Methodologically, we have continuously to reactivate the relationship between living labour, as it is in the here and now, and this hinterland of *potenza* that the history of labour enables us to rediscover.

New figures of capital: global money

Let us return to the main argument. *The expropriation of cooperation is realized by collective capital within the framework of globalized enterprise.* Thus exploitation is, first of all, the reduction of 'cooperative activity' to 'wage labour', and of 'language' to 'language subject to command'. This brings us up against an indefinite series of paradoxes, in which the relationship between the labour of the individual and social productivity is always contradictory, and yet forcefully unified. On the one hand, the reduction of the hours of the working day (or at least of the regulated working day) but, on the other, the indefinite extension of the time of labour (since in this condition the brain also works productively during phases and periods of rest from labour); on the one hand, the apology and the exasperation of command over concrete labour and, on the other, the reference to the socialization of labour, both spatial (mobility) and temporal (flexibility), as the definitive scenario of capitalist creation of value; on the one hand, the affirmation of property-owning individualism, on the other, processes of advanced financialization which dissolve every labourist and Lockeian characteristic of property. The *common* character of productive cooperation and language is caught in a tug-of-war between the private and the public, between the right to private appropriation and the acknowledgement of its public socialization. The bridging of this sharp contradiction, which is necessary for capital to be able to re-impose the mark of exploitation within the globalized enterprise, is constructed (in its more effective figure) through the financialization of the economy. The processes of financialization, and their hidden logic, construct the figure in which collective capital today presents itself, or rather the place 'where blows the breeze of its present efficacy' – to quote Benjamin. Financialization dissolves the traditional characteristics of capitalist society, but reaffirms their dominion at world-wide level.

Thus the methodological *Einleitung* has to open itself to a new object, to the hegemony of the financial markets and to a monetary function which has become as universal as the market. We are immersed in the conspiracy of money, we are prisoners of (and we are at the same time constituted by) this new nature. The qualitative leap (and the 'paradox' – which is a better way of describing it than Marx's 'enigma') consists in the fact that money (this money of the real subsumption of general intellect) has become a representation of that which is the common of life. On the one hand, 'general equivalent', and, on the other, a *dispositif* over future labour; in any case, money presents itself as the artificial form in which common life is definitively given. At this level of development, finance capital is the *volonté générale* of the waged citizens of the world. But this new common substance is traversed by command. Articulating itself between 'general equivalent' and *dispositif* over future labour, the essence of monetary command here becomes apparent in all its purity. Monetary subordination, or rather subjugation, is not simply tied to the exploitation of labour time, but also invests the whole lifetime in this way.

A first brief methodological summary

The theory of value, as we have indicated several times, implies a method of reasearch. In his *Einleitung* of 1857, Marx says that method and the theory of value are two branches of the same tree. So what are the new elements of method which correspond to the new situation of capitalism? We can outline them summarily here, before going on to define them more precisely in the course of our analysis. So we shall say that our method must guide us, first, in moving *between* the productive and the product, the concrete and the abstract, the subjective and the objective, the constructive and the instituted. In the postmodern dimension of production, we find that the *between* is a fundamental terrain of analysis. Then, secondly, the method will allow us to deploy the full potentialities of the concept of living labour, ranging from material determinations to those that are immaterial, relational and expressive, cooperative and scientific. Our method, already located at the intersection of the subjective and the objective, will be able to lead us into the *Darstellung* (exposition) of the figures within which living labour constructs the totality of production. At this point the movement of living labour becomes a machine which is productive of new anthropological figures: human beings inserted within the common production process, the constituent singularities of the multitude, are *hybrid complexities*, biopolitical concatenations, new flesh of the world. Thirdly, our method will enable us to grasp, in all its ambiguity but also in its effectiveness, the productive and transformative *causality of the social movements*. It renews itself continuously in antagonism, and it extends through all the forms of life and production. The lived world reveals itself, in this perspective, as a fabric traversed both by struggles and by the accumulation of the products of living labour: the clarification of the more subtle ramifications of the lived world reveals its dynamics. Fourthly and finally, there is also a kind of 'final cause' (an implicit or latent teleology) that method can reveal. There is nothing predetermined here, but it is a fact that the drive towards the constitution of common goods and towards the new (metamorphic) production of subjectivity is present within this development. There is a kind of *tendency*, like a constitutive drive, which is untimely, yes, but strong: the action of a *cupiditas*. In short, method in postmodernity, compared with method in Marx, is adept at moving on the inside of the existing totality, it is completely immanent, it knows no *outside* but it does know exception, and – when it constructs it – *purpose*.

A biopolitics of general intellect

Let us go back for a moment and look once again at the distance we are taking from Marx. Value, in classic theory from Smith through Ricardo to Marx, has always been considered an expression of labour. Marx saw labour as being definable and measurable in terms of homogenous quantities of time. In Marx himself, however, the unilinear definition of the measure of labour through units of time began to be surpassed when, having set it alongside the problem of the increase of the productivity of labour and of the importance assumed within it by complex labour, he saw the scientific and cooperative dimensions of labour as an original or creative element, which in any event was *excedent* in the determination of value. The measurement of labour by means of homogenous and linear units of time therefore began to be overtaken. We live now in an age in which the cooperative relations of social production and the virtuous accumulation of scientific elements, not to mention the linguistic *dispositif* of productive activity, go to increase the productivity of labour and to strengthen exceptionally its capacity for the transformation of nature and the invention of new being: *today we live at the apogee of a cooperative and scientific practice of the* potenza *of labour.*

Having said that and having made the point about the scientific and cooperative dimensions of the nature of labour, we now have to define *in specific terms* the concept and reality of labour as it stands today. To do this we need to remember that the new relationship between capital and labour opens onto a new phase in the *division of labour*. Marx noted that, tendentially, *in this new phase* 'the development of fixed capital indicates to what degree general social knowledge has become a *direct force of production*, and to what degree, hence, *the conditions of the process of social life itself* [our italics] have come under the control of general intellect and been transformed in accordance with it.' (*Grundrisse*, pp. 706–7). If in fact, following the *Grundrisse*, we call production (which has assumed immaterial labour as the centre and tendency of development) a general intellect, we should add that production through general intellect can in no sense be considered on the basis of an economicist reduction of labour (in *Capital*, cooperation and science were considered solely from the economic point of view, that is, in the calculation of quantitative effects). So we need to change register. Thus we say that in postmodern society *the value of labour presents itself in a biopolitical form*. What does this mean? It means that value is no longer in any sense analysable and measurable in simple quantities of time, and not even in complex sequences, since living and producing have become one single whole, and the time of life and the time of production have become increasingly hybridized. When we refer to *biopolitics*, we mean that life is completely invested by artificial conditions and actions of reproduction, we mean that nature itself has been socialized and has become a productive machine. Labour, in this scenario, becomes completely redefined. And even if we wanted to continue to relate to the old image of a labour that becomes productive only through technological and material dimensions, and in consequence to assert that its greater *potenza* rests simply on complexity, we would nevertheless have to introduce somewhere an *irreducible element of innovation* which goes beyond the simple force of complexity or, rather, offers the same *potenza* as that of a word which acts within a discourse, a name which operates within language – *biopolitical productive cooperation* has by now become *linguistic* and *linguistic community has become productive*. (Naturally, this is a metaphor, but it is a metaphor of a dynamic analogy, of a homology that is tendentially coming into being. We can say that language, once subsumed by machinery, humanizes the machine by which, in turn, it is deeply transformed. The 'linguistic turn', in the world of machinery, will have to be renewed many times until the machine is completely reconquered by human activity, that is, until 'the principal fixed capital becomes man himself' – *Marx dixit* – but fixed capital will itself be different, and man with it.)

Moving from metaphor to the concrete analysis of production, the leap in quality in the new reality of production turns out to be very clear, since the immaterial and scientific dimensions of the processes of value-creation today present themselves by means of *hybridizations* of the various parts of productive activity, as if labour were now formed by a chemistry of different elements (intellectual, material, organizational, artistic, of study and consumption, reproductive and so on): the hard work and creativity of cooperative activity has by now reached an extraordinary effectiveness. Further consequences could be drawn from these premises. In particular, *constant capital* will present itself ever more clearly as a variable dependent on the processes of cooperation of the workforce. Furthermore, at this point (in a manner closely tied to the categories of constant capital) the spectral figure of the commodity can be understood here far better than from reading Book One of Marx's *Capital*. While commodity fetishism is born from the concealment of the social character of the labour which produced that commodity, this concealment could here be extended to all the effects of the mechanism of the production and circulation of commodities, to the production of 'brands', to the slavery produced by exploitation in global outsourcing. The fetishistic character of the commodity has become a 'logo', or rather 'logo' has now become one of the most pertinent definitions of *capital*. Fetish, spectre, fetishistic appropriation, a parasitic place in the organization of social labour. It will appear as the contrary of life. 'Thus the old view, in which the human appears as the aim of production, regardless of his limited national, religious, political character, seems to be very lofty when contrasted to the modern world, where production appears as the aim of mankind and wealth as the aim of production. [. . .] In bourgeois economics – and in the epoch of production to which it corresponds – this complete working-out of the human content appears as total alienation, and the tearing-down of all limited, one-sided aims as sacrifice of the human end-in-itself to an entirely external end.' (*Grundrisse*, pp. 487–8).

Appendix

'In fact, however, when the limited bourgeois form is stripped away, what is wealth other than the universality of human needs, capacities, pleasures, productive forces etc., created through universal exchange? The full development of human mastery over the forces of nature, those of so-called nature as well as of humanity's own nature? The absolute working-out of his creative potentialities, with no presupposition other than the previous historical development, which makes this totality of development, i.e. the development of all human powers as such, the end in itself, not as measured on a *predetermined* yardstick? Where he does not reproduce himself in one specificity, but produces his totality? Strives not to remain something he has become, but is in the absolute movement of becoming?' (*Grundrisse*, p. 488). This is not Lukács, or Bloch, or Benjamin, or any other utopian of the 1920s: it is Marx again, on the same page as the section quoted above. Here the utopia is generic, and nourished by the dialectical illusion of progress and the realization of the totality. We reject this mechanism: but beginning again from the start in weaving the thread of our method does not mean going backwards. We share Marx's faith in the constitutive *potenza* of the method.

The exploitation of *bios*

So what is it, then, this surplus value extracted from the irreducible concatenation of the social production of value? Will it still be possible to explain exploitation in terms of the surplus value produced by the individual and to define it as appropriation, whether public or private, of a part of that which is produced by a mass of individuals? If value is created by common production, it is obvious that on this particular point Marx's theory needs to be modified. Exploitation will mean the appropriation of a part or all of the value that has been constructed *in common*. (This 'in common' does not mean that, in production, workers and bosses stand together: absolutely not! The class struggle continues! The emergence of the common which takes place in the process of production does not eliminate the *antagonism* internal to production but develops it – directly – over the whole of productive society. Workers and capitalists clash *within* social production, because the workers (the multitude) represent the common (cooperation) while the capitalists (power) represent the multiple – but always ferocious – ways of private appropriation.)

And not even this is enough. As well as passing through the appropriation of common value (a process which by now characterizes the mechanism of biopolitical intervention), the rule of exploitation will also pass through the *hierarchical articulation of the biopolitical fabric*, in other words through operations of belonging and exclusion that develop in, and become increasingly more organic to, the mechanism of production. Obviously this definition of exploitation should be understood no longer solely in synchronic, punctual fashion, within specific production processes; it also has to be assumed as a *normative machine* which operates within globalization: in play here are the processes of the *international division of labour* at the level of general intellect; what is in question is the *biopolitical dispositifs* of the global market (of government). The theory of Empire is the new capitalist theory of the division of labour, and *also its critique*.

Biopolitical exploitation is, therefore, an intervention on the flesh of the multitude. This flesh is hybrid: it is hybrid in cultural, productive and linguistic terms; it is, to use the image employed by Democritus and the classical materialists, a seething infinity, a universe of atoms in motion . . . From Prigogine to Donna

Haraway, we have had formidable new descriptions of the *hybrid flesh* of the multitude. And it is not only chemistry or the natural sciences that offer us examples of hybridization: by now the term hybrid has become a constant of our daily imagination. So, given this background, how can we arrive at a full definition of the experience of exploitation in *bios*? We have already said: in terms of exclusion and isolation. Now we can add that *exploitation* becomes, in this scenario, *a de-fleshing of* being. In other words, the *new division of labour* is conducted entirely along lines that are internal to the global labour force, within the borders governed by the owning and managerial powers of the big multinationals and nation-states (powers which, in relation to Empire, are still endowed with a residual strength). The chain of value, after the discovery that it had *a common* substance, must be materially inscribed in *sequences of place* and must be governed by *one single* property-owning command. This control system of cooperation sometimes starts from above and ends below; at other times, it starts from below and ends up above; it always consists in breaking cooperation and turning it into a hierarchical articulation or interaction within a productive system characterized by continuous command. The new communication technologies are fundamental in this process since, as they introduce high efficiency into the interactive coordination between autonomous workers, they nevertheless permit their hierarchical subordination on a property-owning basis.

In these conditions, the exploited are the poor. *But who are the poor?* They are nothing other than the flesh of production, a basic element of biopolitical production, the ambiguous but nonetheless real substance of productive life. The poor person is the excluded one, where, in a situation of common production, every subject is included within the world of production. Many people say that the cooperative system inevitably has to bring about a terminal contradiction with the physical, property-based capitalist system; and that all that is left for us, today, is to verify the contradiction. It will be also true that global knowledge and cooperation in general intellect will inevitably put seriously to the test that new division of labour on which exploitation is being installed today: but, for us, the objective tendency is not enough. There is a subject who is central in the determination of antagonism, and that is the poor. The poor – both the excluded and the included

– the exploited (even if they don't work, but simply because they participate in society). But also, the poor are the salt of the earth because, while the rich person always has a place, the poor are always uprooted, even when they are in a place, singular in all the movements of their exodus. 'This living labour, existing as an abstraction from these moments of its actual reality (also, not-value); this complete denudation, purely subjective existence of labour, stripped of all objectivity. Labour as *absolute poverty*; poverty not as shortage, but as total exclusion of objective wealth. Or also as the existing *not-value*, and hence purely objective use value, existing without mediation, this objectivity can only be an objectivity not separated from the person; only an objectivity coinciding with his immediate bodily existence.' (*Grundrisse*, pp. 295–6). But this definition of the poor can also turn into something positive: 'Labour not as an object, but as activity; not as itself *value*, but as the *living source* of value. [Namely, it is] general wealth (in contrast to capital in which it exists objectively, as reality) as the general possibility of the same, which proves itself as such in action . . . . 'Thus, it is not at all contradictory . . . that labour is *absolute poverty as object*, on one side, and is, on the other side, the *general possibility of wealth* as subject and as activity.'(*Grundrisse*, p. 296).

A second brief summary on method

Here, therefore, Marx's *Einleitung* needs to be renewed. In notebook M of the *Grundrisse*, one of the fundamental points was the demonstration that, when production comes to dominate the entire process of social life, when real subsumption becomes a reality, the method of political economy can itself be based on a tendency, which becomes increasingly pronounced, of labour to become abstract, to define itself as a universal genus: within this form, all working activities can be unified. Today we are in a position where we can understand this methodological development and take it much further than was possible for Marx. Marx had to assume in his basic protocol that 'the concrete is concrete because it is the concentration of many determinations, hence unity of the diverse' (*Grundrisse*, p. 101). In his *Einleitung*, he expressed it as follows: 'indifference towards specific labours corresponds to a form of society in which individuals can with ease transfer from one labour to another, and where the specific kind is a matter of chance for them, hence of indifference. Not only the category labour, but labour in reality has here become the means of creating wealth in general, and has ceased to be organically linked with particular individuals in any specific form. Such a state of affairs is at its most developed in the most modern forms of existence of bourgeois society – in the United States. Here, then, for the first time, the point of departure of modern economics, namely the abstraction of the category 'labour', 'labour as such', labour pure and simple, becomes true in practice. (*Grundrisse*, pp. 104–5). For us, the situation is different: the concrete is no longer simply *a synthesis of determinations* but rather a *multiplicity of singularities related to the common*; the concrete is the common name: thus, beyond the point of view of *Capital*, a proliferation of common labour.

But again, this is not enough: Marx adds that 'production thus produces not only an object for the subject, but also a subject for the object' (*Grundrisse*, p. 92). It is around this statement that the *Einleitung* reaches its higher point – when the objective analysis of capitalist development (which has laid the basis of a biopolitical vision of exploitation) shifts us towards subjectivity, in other words towards the point at which subjectivity produces innovation and makes labour fertile through cooperation. Now, this is also the point in which the capacity of the poor is realized, and of the worker, and of the excluded, and of the exploited (we could have said, of the *de-fleshed*) – their capacity for revolt. This first topological approach to postmodern exploitation places us in the condition of imagining revolt at the point where innovation, the creation of new value, are given – in any case, to imagine research as desire, or, better, as a trajectory of incarnation. Freedom seeks to make itself body: common bodies of cooperation, multiple bodies of general intellect, bodies of antagonism.

Index